# MISBEHAVING IN MAINE

# MISBEHAVING IN MAINE

30 Half-Learned Lessons

**DAN WILLIAMS**

FALLS CITY PRESS
Beaver Falls, Pennsylvania

www.fallscitypress.com

MISBEHAVING IN MAINE: 30 HALF-LEARNED LESSONS
©2025 Falls City Press by Dan Williams

2108 Seventh Avenue
Beaver Falls, PA 15010
www.fallscitypress.com

All rights reserved. Except for brief quotations in printed reviews, no part of this book may be reproduced, stored, or transmitted by any means without prior written permission of the publisher.

All websites listed herein are accurate as of the date of publication but may change in the future. The inclusion of a website does not indicate the promotion of the entirety of the website's content.

Art by Dan Williams
Cover Design by Kristen Slebodnik

---

Library of Congress Cataloging-in-Publication Data

Williams, Daniel, 1981—

    p. cm.
  Includes bibliographical references.

Identifiers:
  ISBN: 978-1-7369184-9-4

Subjects: LCSH: Williams, Daniel, 1981– | Humorists, American — 21st century — Biography. | American wit and humor — 21st century. | Maine — Social life and customs — Humor. | Memoirs. | I. Title.

PN6231.H8 W55 2025

---

*Printed in the United States of America*

# Contents

| | |
|---|---|
| Lesson 1: That Tickle in Your Throat Might be a Nation | 1 |
| Lesson 2: It Isn't Necessarily A Good Thing When Your Mother Dances | 7 |
| Lesson 3: Lying Can Bring Us Together | 17 |
| Lesson 4: If Someone on Sesame Street Orders You to Pee Your Pants, You Do It | 27 |
| Lesson 5: Sometimes the Thoughts in Your Head Are From Your Big Brother The Devil | 35 |
| Lesson 6: The More You Love *Star Wars*, The More They Can Hurt You | 43 |
| Lesson 7: If You Want Your Parents' Attention, Run Over Something They Love | 51 |
| Lesson 8: Your Balls are Just Balls, But Gremlins are Forever | 59 |
| Lesson 9: You Can Steal Your Brother's Sin, But You Can't Steal His Glory | 67 |
| Lesson 10: Occasionally, Violence Isn't the Way | 79 |
| Lesson 11: You Never Forget Your First F-Bomb | 91 |
| Lesson 12: Parents Who Don't Force Musical Instruments on Their Children Deny Them the Profound Pleasure of Quitting | 107 |
| Lesson 13: Not Everyone Should Be Allowed to Draw Your Face | 113 |
| Lesson 14: There is a God on Frozen Ponds | 119 |
| Lesson 15: When Your Great Aunt Asks if You Want to See Her Surgery, What Choice Do You Have? You're a Kid | 125 |
| Lesson 16: If You Have a Song to Sing, Sing it. Damn the Danger | 137 |

Lesson 17: Older Brothers Giveth, But Not Without First Taketching a Lot Away 143

Lesson 18: There's No Such Thing as an Unconditional Crush 153

Lesson 19: Attempted Murder Doesn't Make You a Failure. At Least You Tried, Which is More Than Most People Can Say 163

Lesson 20: Grandparents Can, in Fact, Run. You Just Have to Get Them Mad Enough 175

Lesson 21: You Shouldn't Kill Your Little Sister, Even if She'd Go Along With it Just to Be With You 183

Lesson 22: A Kid Who Eats His Shoes Often Has a Pretty Good Reason 193

Lesson 23: The Road to Heaven May Be Rough, But It Isn't Hell 205

Lesson 24: Teachers Have Emotions Too, and Pasts, and Were Once Young, and Can Feel Pain 215

Lesson 25: If You Want to Meet an Axe Murderer, Look No Further Than the Boy Next Door 225

Lesson 26: To Discover How Much a Girl Really Likes You, Ruin Your Life Right in Front of Her 243

Lesson 27: There is *Everything* to Be Afraid of in the Dark 259

Lesson 28: You Can Ruin Biology with Your Chemistry 269

Lesson 29: It's So Easy to Lose Friends, There Shouldn't Be Any Friends Left 281

Lesson 30: There's More Than Sound and Fury in a Homemade Bomb: Sometimes, There's Love. In Other Words, the End of War 289

To My Mindy, the Story Queen.

# LESSON 1:

# That Tickle in Your Throat Might be a Nation

When my great-grandfather William Williams was a boy, a boy named at a time when words were few and worth repeating, he stood with his mother on the Southampton docks. They had third-class tickets to get from England to America by ship. This was April 1912.

Guess which ship.

As they waited, William Williams' mother had one rule: "Do *not* cough."

I'll explain in a second. But first, consider William's mother:

Imagine a severe woman, born in a black dress. She's tall, bonneted, and pissed.

In other words, she's Whistler's mother from that painting *Whistler's Mother*.

But *standing*.

Go look at the painting. If *that* woman stood up, you would run. Yes, you would. Picture a seven-foot mother in a strangling mood, a mother ducking through your bedroom doorway, her long fingers dragging on the hardwood.

*That's* who was leaning down to say to William Williams,

"*DO NOT COUGH!*"

Why not? Here's why:

In those old times, everyone was on the lookout for a certain kind of cough: the pertussis cough. It's the kind that makes you whoop, so they called it "whooping cough." It was a real killer (still is), and if you had it, you got banned from coffee houses, posses, opium dens, public executions, and you certainly didn't get to die on the Titanic, no matter how third-class you were.

And though William Williams didn't have whooping cough, he did have a cough that day which sounded a lot like a whoop.

He tried his hardest to obey Mother, who suggested, "Don't breathe." He didn't, until he did, and he did it while they were halfway up the boarding ramp. He breathed and coughed:

"Whoop!"

Instantly, the boarding agent at the bottom of the ramp shouted something in British: "Oi!"

Mother hissed at William Williams, "Keep going!"

Another official, this one guarding the top of the ramp, also shouted, "Oi!" which roughly translates to, "You've got a whooping boy. No Titanic for you!"

And so it was: My relatives, the sick and the furious, had to find another way across.

For that, I am forever and ever grateful.

Thank you, coughing boy.

The particles and droplets of your cough are us, the crop of so many names blooming on the Williams' family tree.

You whooped and we flew. We grew.

You whooped, therefore I am.

Yes, I'm thankful, but I'm also scared.

It's scary to know I only exist because of one little innocent cough that slipped from my great-grandfather's mouth.

That's me. That's my people.

The central figure on our coat of arms should be a coughing boy hunching in the shadow of a nine-foot mother whose anger didn't begin to melt until around 2:20 AM on the 15th of April 1912.

Though it scares me, I'm glad my existence hangs on a cough. It makes me remember how easy it is to not be here at all.

Very easy.

It also makes me wonder…

*How many other lucky whoops are in my bloodline back to the beginning?*

I feel so accidental. So eerily random.

I feel like a miracle.

I guess that's not so bad.

your doodles, memories, illustrations, story ideas...

your doodles, memories, illustrations, story ideas...

## LESSON 2:

# It Isn't Necessarily a Good Thing When Your Mother Dances

Thirty-nine years ago, a giant pile of firewood fell and crushed me. There's an awesome scar on my head to prove it. It looks like I got bitten by George Washington's wooden teeth.

There's a weird memory to prove it too.

Though I was buried, I could still see the upper world. The firewood had fallen in a gracious way, giving one of my eyes a crazy, little tunnel so I could see daylight. And in the daylight, out on the green lawn, I saw something I'd never seen before:

My mother...

Dancing.

Dancing on the lawn.

I can explain, but first, let me tell you how I ended up under a winter's worth of firewood.

## The How

Imagine Maine, a place where winter doesn't care that we're in modern times. Nope. It cherishes the old-fashioned tradition of spending one third of every year trying to kill you. You fight winter with fire. Firewood. You get yourself tons of firewood and live.

Now, imagine the stack of firewood beside my old house. It was eight feet tall and twenty feet long. A vertical pallet at each end kept the stack from exploding outward in either direction and killing the children.

But what about the pallets? What kept *them* from exploding outward and killing the children?

Dad stabbed two-by-fours into the ground, then angled them against the pallets as braces. This allowed us to stack high and keep our thousands of pounds of firewood in one place.

I didn't go to the woodpile that day to climb the pile. Woodpiles are dangerous. I went to climb a bracing pallet or two.

The cross pieces and gaps of pallets make them perfect little ladders. I intended to climb, hold on to the top board, then rock my 5-year-old body backwards, jolting the pallet. It wasn't a perfect plan, but a good plan today is better than a perfect plan tomorrow.

I remember exactly what was going through my mind:

I was on the high seas, battling a great storm. And since there were no high seas or great storms around, and no ships, the pallet was my ship, my home, and I was the sea and its storm.

In addition, I was Captain Donald Duck.

Why Donald? Why not Mickey, Goofy, or Pluto?

I don't know. The brain of a five-year-old is a bubbling stew of chaos. A portion of sentient duck must have surfaced in the stew, enough for me to guess the identification of the rest of him. So, that's why.

Gripping the pallet, I threw myself backwards ninety-nine times. Each jolt was a ship-killing wave. Each wave, I survived.

Alone.

Where was my crew? I was young and didn't know I needed crews. Plus, they were all dead. What got them? Whatever else was in the stew: bad weather, madness, krakens, cannibalism, and God's water bullies, the great whales who'd gotten hooked on prophets and now wanted to sample every other kind of person.

My fun?

Significant.

My understanding of cause, effect, and risk?

Nonexistent.

I simply hadn't been alive long enough:

- I was born.
- I learned to walk, talk, and climb.
- Dad stacked wood and braced it with pallets.
- Dad assumed I wasn't a moron.
- I didn't see pallets. I saw my ship.
- I climbed aboard.
- I shook my ship.

That's all I knew.

And I was having the time of my life. I had found my reason to live.

If what happened next hadn't happened next, I'd probably be there still, a 42-year-old man pulling violently on a wood-pile pallet while screaming for joy like a duck.

Unfortunately, what happened did end up happening, and I've been searching for a new reason to live ever since.

As I stormed on, jarring the pallet harder with each wave, its vital two-by-four began losing its grip. It budged centimeter by centimeter, more and more, and *more*, until...

The two-by-four slipped its grip and fell.

And I fell.

And a rogue tsunami of firewood rose up high and higher, blotting out the sun, and *it* fell.

Burying me.

But to be fair to the wood, maybe death was exactly what I needed. At the age of five, I was already showing disquieting signs, the big three:

- Bed-wetting
- Animal cruelty
- And the love of fire

Signs that you just might be a little psychopath in need of a mercy kill.

## ONE: Bed-Wetting

I wet the bed all the time, even when I didn't have to.

I filled my footie pajamas to the knees, giving my legs the look of early onset edema.

Sloshing downstairs for breakfast, I resembled an adventurer trying to load my deep-sea diver's suit with that breathable liquid oxygen the military uses for super deep dives.

As usual, no one was impressed but me.

## TWO: Animal cruelty

I treated Jimmy, my teddy bear, terribly. I withheld affection, never made eye contact, and I forced him to live his life facing a corner until I needed him for punishment.

Why?

Three reasons.

He wasn't a short-hair bear. He had long, scraggly hair all over his body like a wannabe socialist. He was a radical with parasites to conceal. I wanted to give Jimmy a trim, but I couldn't discuss knives with my mother in a way that didn't alarm her.

The second reason I hated my bear was because I was practically born hating the name Jimmy. Sorry to the decent Jimmys out there, but I've just never run into any evidence that they exist. Was it unfair of me to hate Jimmy for his name, a name I'd given him myself? No. He looked like a Jimmy, and that wasn't my fault.

The third reason I hated him: his clothes. They were stitched to his body. I couldn't remove them, so I had no way of delousing him or checking for far worse dangers.

## Far Worse Dangers

When you were five, maybe you learned about the penis of your neighbor's dog, Mr. Hank. What did you maybe learn?

That dog penises were left unfinished by God. Because of this, you likely witnessed the phenomenon known as the "red rocket." When you saw that blood-red worm jousting out of Mr. Hank's friendly, furry penis, you thought he was dying, didn't you?

"No," said your parents, "*all* dogs' penises do that. It's normal."

You then had a new definition of normal. Normal meant something that's totally fine but also possibly conceals the telescoping penis of the Devil.

After the informative chat with your parents, you were on the lookout for red rockets everywhere. If someone had a crotch, you suspected them. You even mistrusted your own friendly penis. You stared into its little black hole, playing chicken with the evil inside you.

## Back To Jimmy

Since I couldn't remove his clothing to check for ticks and abominations, he was never safe. I could never bring myself to cuddle with him or let him share my bed, because days later, while enjoying pasta with the family, something might burst from my chest. I didn't know this back then, of course. I hadn't seen *Alien* yet. I was too young.

But I *felt* it.

## THREE: The Love Of Fire

I adored fire. As I gazed into it, I got blissfully lost. I wanted to hold it, to pet it, and call it my own. Elemental kitty of the bright, red hair, I love you. At birthday parties, I worshiped matches and trick candles: "Blessed art thou among candles, and blessed is the fruit of thy wick, O flame that dieth not." When my grandfather and I watched fire in the fireplace, he said, "See the people dancing?"

"No."

"That's what the flames are. Those are people dancing in there."

"*I* want to dance in there."

I dreamed of heaven, a place filled with fire, and everywhere people were dancing so wildly it looked like pain. Like paradise.

Take me home.

## Bonus Warning Sign

I attempted to kill my sister.

Mom and Dad said she was a gift from God. I waited for them to finish saying this and leave Meg's room for a moment so I could press my face to the bars of her crib like Jack Nicholson and cough.

Into my sister's face, I coughed and coughed the lethal perfume of my dead heart.

All this to say, at the age of five, the spirit animal of my morality was a horse with four broken legs. Death would do me good, and God knew it. Thankfully, he doesn't always use what he knows. Sometimes he uses grace in the form of punishing the living crap out of someone instead of killing them. He is the tough-love shepherd who beats the evil out of his sheep with his crook, saying, "This hurts me more than it hurts you," and the sheep would believe this, but they're sheep, the world's first and foremost knowers of nothing.

So, the firewood fell, and Captain Duck went down with his ship.

I don't remember pain. I don't remember screaming, though I wish I did. I'd like to know if I screamed like Donald Duck. For one, that would be hilarious. For two, my duck scream would tell me how deeply in character I was. A boy who's a duck for the game but not for the pain, that's not so good. That's a thin imagination. But a boy who's a duck for the game *and* the pain, that's a boy who would have been duck enough to die a duck, and *that's* an imagination worth remembering.

As you know, though I was under the woodpile, I could still see. One eyeball sent a trembling flagellum of sight down that crazy vision tunnel in the firewood, which makes me understand what they say: "When God closes a door, he opens a window." They say this even though it makes God sound like he's halfway into burglary. Which half? The scriptures do not tell.

So, I gazed down that crooked, wooden spyglass of a corridor and saw the lawn, and on the lawn, I saw, as you also know…

My mother dancing.

Dancing on the lawn.

*My* mother, who does not dance. She was born and raised in northern Maine, where the winters are so deep and long and cold, if you dance, you die. How come? Because you just wasted firewood gathering time with that little dance experiment of yours. Enjoy dancing with the Devil in hell, silly child.

*That* woman, my mother, dancing.

That's what I thought I saw anyway. What should have changed my mind was her screaming. But it didn't. I'd never seen her dance before. Maybe her dancing had a screaming component. How would I know?

I later learned what scared Mom enough to make her dance and scream was what she saw: One five-year-old foot sticking like a flag of surrender out of 3000 pounds of firewood.

What happened next?

I imagine Mom danced her way over to the pile and began incorporating chunks of wood into her dance, flinging pieces high, making a rooster tail of firewood in the air behind her, gradually exposing her buried boy.

She did all this for me, saving my life, keeping me on Earth despite all those red flags. Flags she knew by heart.

After all, it was Mom who caught me trying to sever Meg's bloodline with a cough, Mom who redirected me again and again from beating Jimmy's face into a dirty countercultural pancake with my fists, and it was Mom who always drained the yellow swelling from my footie pajamas.

Even after all this, she saved me.

Why?

Because she knew what every mother knows:

She knew that children who live, even if they're wicked, can reform.

She knew that as long as there's a minute left of a child's living, that's space enough for an epiphany, an apology, an admission:

"My evil was never your fault, Mother. It was Nature's fault. No amount of nurturing could have erased it. In fact, you're the only reason I wasn't even eviler."

And, at the very least, my mother knew this:

Living children are far better at restacking firewood than children who are dead.

# LESSON 3:

# Lying Can Bring Us Together

When I tell people about my war with my brother, I say, "It was psychological." Joe didn't punch or push or kick...

He talked to me.

He taught me early on that a person is made of words. It's like this: People are ships. Positive words make for light cargos. The ships ride high and happy on the waves. Negative words are heavy cargos, sinking the ships lower and lower. When Joe wanted to sink me, he didn't need fists or feet.

He used words.

Today, he's an electrical engineer. I don't know what that is, so I think of him as a scientist. This makes sense to me because he's been a scientist since childhood.

Here's one of his oldest experiments:

**JOE:** Does this word hurt you?

**DAN:** No.

**JOE:** What about this one?

**DAN:** Yes!

**JOE:** Really? This word here?

**DAN:** Oh, yes! It hurts!

**JOE:** Amazing. (makes a note) What if I combine it with these other words?

**DAN:** Ahhh! That's so much worse!

**JOE:** Fascinating. (makes another note)

**DAN:** Joe?

**JOE:** Yes?

**DAN:** I think I just died on the inside.

**JOE:** (looks at watch) Okay, I'm calling it. At 3:47 p.m., Subject B died on the inside. That's test number 982. Excellent. (makes many notes) Right... I will now revive Subject B and begin test 983.

Sometimes, Joe used words to insult me. Sometimes he used them to critique the way I biked and drew and laughed and breathed and hoped and dreamed, and if I ever died, he'd critique that too. And sometimes, when he was feeling especially scientific, he told destabilizing, horrifying untruths about the world so he could note my reactions.

For example:

One day, Joe and I were standing in the driveway. We had a unique driveway. From the crown of it, you could see everything: miles and miles, all the way to the purple mountains' majesty. On the other side of those mountains? The end of Maine. In other words, the end of the whole world and reality too.

There we stood, checking out the majesty, watching rogue crows cross the sky, looking at smoke-snakes slithering out of faraway chimneys, when Joe said, "You know pterodactyls?"

At the time, I was holding a pterodactyl. "I'm familiar," I said.

"Well, they're still alive."

"What do you mean?"

"Just what I said. They're alive and flying around still."

"Yeah, but not in America."

"Oh yes, in America. *Big time.*"

"Really?"

"*Really.* They could pick you up easy and carry you away. We'd never see you again."

"*No.*"

"*Yes.*"

"How do you know?"

"I just do."

That was good enough for me. I looked frantically to the skies. "This is horrible!"

"I know. And for you it's *really* horrible."

"Why?"

"See, I'm much too big to pick up, but you're exactly the right size. They can spot you a mile away, and when they come to get you, you never hear them. You don't even *see* them. They fly just above the trees. And right before they get you, there's a huge shadow on the ground all around you. You look up, and there it is. A *pterodactyl*. It grabs you with its long claws then carries you away, and that's the last anyone ever sees you. It happens all the time. *Especially* in America."

And with that, the sky changed.

*I* changed.

I had formerly been a boy who worried only about ghosts and Satan and bears and murderous marijuana farmers deep in the woods. Now, dinosaurs were on my list. My darling dinosaurs. I looked at the pterodactyl in my hand. He was just a baby. I looked at the sky again and imagined his mother. From a mile away, she sees two boys. One she ignores. He's much too big. The other, however, is small, the perfect size for carrying and killing. With one easy swing of her long, leather wings, she rises then flies, covering that mile in seconds, soaring mere feet above the leafy canopy, keeping out of sight. The trees open for a driveway where the two boys stand. She dives, eclipsing the sun. Her shadow's as big as an airplane, and her body's silent as a cloud. Before the smaller boy knows what's happening, her long fingers wrap around him in a crushing grip then tear him screaming up into the wild and unsympathetic blue yonder.

I imagined these things until a crow in a nearby tree screamed. I screamed and ran crying for the house. Joe ran after me, and for some reason he was trying to stop me from sharing with Mom the awful truth about prehistoric death in the skies.

It was back!

Tearfully, I told, screaming, "They're back! They're back!"

"Who's back?" said Mom.

"DINOSAURS! I'm dead! You and Joe are much too heavy to lift, but I'M DEAD!"

Mom punished Joe, and though she told me the truth about pterodactyls, it still took a while for the air to clear of their presence, and longer for them to leave my dreams.

But looking back, I'm grateful. How many people can say they know what it feels like to be hunted by a dinosaur? *I* can. And this experience has helped prepare me for adulthood, that time in life when we're increasingly aware that no day is safe. Our end can come at any time, from anywhere, even the sky on a clear, blue day. We begin to sense we're being watched, followed, hunted by something inevitable, an ancient, monstrous, silent fact. When it dives down into the clearing where we're standing, no matter how hard we run, we'll never make it home.

Every day that I'm not carried away screaming into the sky, never to be seen again, is a good day.

Thank you, Joe. In the end, it was a good lie, and I'm grateful.

A month after my taste of Mesozoic hell, Joe and I were on a hill in the woods. My father called the hill "Birch Mountain" because it was a high hill with birches on it. Also, it was on our property, and though owning hills is great, owning mountains is better.

Joe was weaving dead branches into a lean-to. I was in the tree the lean-to was leaning on. As I gazed off into the empty blue distances, I had an idea.

"Joe," I said, and when I said it, I made myself sound scared. "*Joe.*"

He didn't answer.

I tried to sound even more scared. "*Joe!*"

"What?"

"There's a *bear.*"

"What?"

"A bear! There's a black bear!"

He lowered the branch he was holding. "No there isn't."

"It's in the swamp," I said. There was a swamp at the bottom of the mountain. "It's in the swamp at the bottom of the mountain. It's climbing! It's coming toward us!"

"There's no bear," he said, though if he really believed this, he would have gone back to his lean-to weavings. He did not. He dropped the branch. Then he looked down the mountain toward the swamp. He could see nothing because you can see nothing when you're standing on Birch Mountain. You can hardly even see the mountain. There's too much brush, too many birches in the way. But if you're in a tree, like I was, you see everything, sometimes even things that aren't there at all.

"Yes, there *is* a bear!" I said. "It's big!"

"Is there really?" Now *he* sounded scared. And that scared me. My belief-meter suddenly registered a pulse. It was weak, but it was there. I looked down into the brush and birches of the mountainside, I looked to the swamp, searching frantically for bears, real ones.

Joe and I had been taught all our lives to fear bears, because when Maine isn't trying to kill you with winter, that's what it uses: bears. And when neither of those things work, it settles for seasonal affective disorder and depression, things which are basically winter and bears *on the inside*.

Once, our father crept up on us in the woods while we were playing with a deer skeleton or shoving sticks into a hole in the ground, a bee hole. Dad charged from behind a tree, screaming, "ROAR!!!" and all three of us died. Joe and I died of fear. Dad died of laughter. But he'd earned it for teaching us a good lesson: vigilance. Maine's bears (black bears) are no joke. They kill children, especially those who believe in them. And they don't kill like grizzlies, which is sometimes fast. They kill *slow*. They dig at your belly with their long claws, digging for every last scrap of your blood and meat, and for the vast, hidden deposits of candy, which bears prize above all else. It can take weeks.

"Are you lying?!" Joe cried.

"I'm *not* lying!" A lie, yes, though again, my fear was somewhat real, about 1 to 2 percent real, and when you're in the woods, that's plenty. "It's climbing the mountain! Run! You have to run! NOW!"

He spent a few more seconds trying to see if he could spot this gigantic bear who was somehow raging our way silently through the underbrush and deep, dead leaves, which are traditionally extremely loud things when under the feet of bears.

"Hurry!" I yelled.

And Joe did hurry, but instead of running away home, he ran for a tree. The nearest one. My tree. He jumped to the lowest branch then climbed. He climbed higher and higher, as fast as he could, breathing heavily, groaning with fear as he climbed, and in between all the huffing, puffing, and groaning, he managed to say, "You... better... not be... lying."

It was fun to see him climb so fast, great that he was afraid, and that I had made it happen. *Me*. Mr. Gullible. The lightweight. The powerless. But as he got closer, I started to realize that the only dangerous animal who was *actually* in the area one hundred percent was Joe, and he was climbing right toward the high branches where I perched.

He stopped just beneath me and looked around. "Where is it?"

I pretended to be looking everywhere for bear and bear-sign, and was doing a good job until I accidentally let a smile slip out from beneath my bear-seeking expression. It spoiled my act.

"You *lied*," Joe said.

I lied again: "No! I thought I saw a bear!"

"You're a *liar*."

I should have said, "This seems like a convenient time to talk about pterodactyls." Instead, I said, "No I'm not. I really thought I saw a bear!"

And that's when he said it: "I hate you."

It hurt to hear this.

It was the evilest thing we knew how to say back then, this being before we learned Hindi

from *Indiana Jones and the Temple of Doom*. I remember drying dishes once and passing the time by using the movie's foreign phrases to open a dialogue with Kali, the Hindu goddess of death.

"What are you saying?" Dad asked, looking a little alarmed.

"Nothing."

"Well, *stop* it."

"Okay," I said, in English, then I did what all kids do: I tucked my Hindi away and went to my room where I could chat with Kali in peace.

But before *The Temple of Doom*, "I hate you" was our most forbidden bit of language. I remember Joe stomping up the stairs once after an altercation with Mom. He paused to turn back and say, "I hate you," then he continued on his way.

He didn't get far.

There was a sudden explosion of fatherly sound and movement. Dad moved so fast in his pursuit of Joe it was small-town teleportation. He grabbed Joe and carried him downstairs in his arms like a cursed baby, then he held Joe trembling in the air in front of Mom until something shivered out of Joe that sounded like, "I'm sorry."

*I hate you* was just something we didn't say.

So, when Joe said it, I said, "I'm telling."

"Then *I'll* tell that you *lied*."

"You lied about pterodactyls!"

This gave him pause. Then it made him smile. "And *you* believed it."

"*You* believed about the bear."

"Not really," he said.

"Yes, you *did!* You were scared!"

"No, I wasn't."

"Yes, you *were!*"

We fought. We called each other babies and idiots. "You're stupid." "You're a freak." We called each other liars, and it was true.

But we also stayed in that tree.

We stayed, even though Joe hated me, and the lean-to wasn't finished; even though the tree was uncomfortable and getting worse; and even though I'd made up the bear, and we both knew it, we stayed where we were, balancing on branches, fighting.

Eventually we got to talking. This led to laughing. And behind it all, maybe we were thinking, *Let's stay up here a little longer. Just in case. If there* is *a bear, after all, we'll be safer in a tree.*

*We'll be safer if we stick together.*

## LESSON 4:

# If Someone on Sesame Street Orders You to Pee Your Pants, You Do It

How old am I? I am 1, 2, 3, 4, 5, 6, 7, 8, 9, or 10, and I'm very into Sesame Street. An argument could be made for 11, 12, and 13 too.

I close my eyes, fall asleep, and when I open my eyes, I'm in a dream. I'm sitting on the front steps I love most, steps I watch and need every day. You guessed it: the steps of 123 Sesame Street, that famous apartment building with the green front door and the homeless monster living just outside.

Ah, New York City.

Two adults, Gordon and Maria, are present in the dream. They're teaching me and two other children a lesson about counting, a lesson already in progress when I arrive.

Gordon says, "One, two, three."

The kids repeat this. I catch on fast and join them for "three."

Then Maria pipes up: "And what do we do on the count of three?"

I have no idea, but the other kids seem to know. They raise their hands and are bouncing up and down, fidgeting, bursting at the seams with the pressure of having the right answer.

Maria smiles. "Yes, Becky? Yes, Joey?"

Little Becky and Joey shout, "At the count of three, we *pee!*"

I expect Maria to lose it: "Are you *nuts*? We *never* pee outdoors on Sesame Street!"

"Who's *we*?" says the peeing, homeless monster.

However, Maria doesn't lose it. So maybe we *will* be peeing after all, or at least she and Gordon will teach us a lesson about it, define it, maybe, show us how the pee is made. But that's more of a Mr. Rogers thing.

Gordon and Maria are smiling. *Big.* And they're starting to act just like the kids. They're bouncing up and down, fidgeting, bursting. I'm doing it too, or rather my body is doing it, doing its best to hang on to something.

Then Gordon and Maria shock me.

Together, they say, "That's right! We sure do pee! On the count of three, we *all* pee!" and everyone cheers.

But I don't cheer. I'm still in shock.

Gordon and Maria stop wiggling and glare at me. They appear to be confused by my shock, my non-cheering. And their enthusiasm, trapped inside them because I didn't clap or cry out with happiness, seems to be giving them pains, cramps maybe.

Their eyes say, "Who is this rogue who doesn't know enough to celebrate good things? Where'd he come from, and who the hell told him how to get, how to get to, Sesame Street?"

Their disgusted faces scare me. Will Gordon and Maria become aggressive? Will they attack like white blood cells, eliminating the foreign invader from their street, maybe wheel out a garbage can for me to cool my heels in until I can get with the program?

I begin to wiggle more violently, hoping to camouflage myself in the company of Joey and Becky who wiggle like they're on fire. I bop up and down in a submissive display of excitement that would probably look like physical discomfort if I wasn't smiling so hard, smiling to hide my fear of Gordon and Maria. And, to be honest, I *am* a little physically uncomfortable. I snuck thirty-five gulps of apple juice thirty-five seconds before bed, though I don't remember this now. I don't remember anything from my other life. All I know is Sesame Street, these steps, this kid Joey, that kid Becky, Gordon and Maria, the nearby monster who hasn't stopped peeing since I got here, and the counting game I'm caught up in, the game that ends in violating a social norm.

Slowly but surely, Gordon and Maria stop scowling at me and go back to bopping and squirming. Then they start squeezing their knees together and crossing their legs this way and that.

Suddenly, Gordon says, "Is everybody ready?"
Wisely I cheer with the other children: "Yes! Yaaaay!"
"On the count of three…" says Maria.
Gordon holds up a single finger. "One!"
Joey, Becky, and I sing out, "One!"
Maria holds up two fingers. "Two!"
"Two!" we shout.

Gordon and Maria say, "THREE!"

Joey, Becky, and I wave our arms around and point our faces to the sky. "Three!"

Then we all cry out in one great voice, "We pee!"

What did I do at this point?

What *could* I do?

I was with Gordon, Maria, Joey, Becky, and a nonconformist monster on Sesame Street without my parents. In other words, I was on my own. The only authorities anywhere were Gordon and Maria, trusted powerhouses reinforced by Mother daily when she turned on the TV and said, "Sit," and "Watch," and "Don't move until this is *done*," and Gordon and Maria had given me a direct order.

Again, what could I do?

Sesame Street taught me to read and count. It taught me to put my life in the hands of enormous birds. It showed math has meaning, but only if you sing it. On the steps of 123, I learned cooperation, sharing, and reconciliation strategies. Then came my dream. Suddenly my Sesame education rounded an astonishing bend and taught me something completely surprising. But that's what good education does. It surprises you.

Surprise: I now knew what we do after three:

"One… Two… Three… We PEE!!!"

And I did.

With Gordon and Maria, I peed. With Joey, Becky, and the monster, I let fly. Pee pooled and ran down the steps of 123 in a decorative waterfall of relief. Not my pee, though. Mine didn't run down the stairs, adding hints of apple to the other aromas. Mine poured into my footie pajamas, warming my feet, warming all of me and whispering away the tightness of the bowling ball my belly had become. As easy as 1, 2, 3, I filled my accurately named P.J.'s. I filled them up, up, and up some more. Like education fills the willing mind, I filled them to the happy, tippy top.

It's been many years since that dream. Many other authorities have overshadowed Gordon and Maria in my mind.

And yet…

I wonder now and then what would happen if I found myself once more on the steps of 123 with the old team.

I can see it.

The kids are grown now. Joey's seventy-seven. Becky's eighty. I'm eighty-two. The monster's a hundred and thirteen, a medical miracle. How did he manage it? He claims he uses "spite."

Everyone is old but Gordon and Maria. They are somehow young. They look amazing! Time has been fabulous to them, and they know it. They're beaming. They're wiggling and fidgeting with joy.

By the light in their eyes, I can tell they're excited to teach the lesson they have for us today. Their eyes glow like sunlight on so much water. It's the look of loving your job, of knowing your purpose and living to fulfill it. It's the look of two Sesame Street veterans on the verge of counting.

Joey, Becky, and I begin to bop and writhe like our teachers, and though it's a stretch these days, we cross our rheumatic legs tightly. We cross them the other way.

A timeless voice from the trashcan asks, "What are you waiting for?"

Everyone smiles. There are no authorities now, only friends. Still, Gordon and Maria teach. They ask us to hold hands. We do.

They say, "One."
We say, "One."
They say, "Two."
We say, "Two."
They say "Three…" and so do we.

After that, no one says another word. We don't need to. We've lived too much and too long to spell it all out. "Three" has become a shorthand among soldiers. It means we all pause for a moment, remembering ancient rhymes and songs and lessons learned, and then we all leap together into a freedom so old and yet as close and warm as yesterday.

This is the power of Sesame Street.

Holding the hands of friends, equals, our inhibitions have gone so very far away. My heart is full, all of me, full to the tippy top.

I close my eyes.

I let go.

I feel like a kid again.

your doodles, memories, illustrations, story ideas...

# LESSON 5:

# Sometimes the Thoughts in Your Head Are From Your Big Brother The Devil

My aunt, a school bus driver long ago, occasionally parked the bus in Grammy and Grampa's driveway over the weekend. School buses are safe on the weekend, which is why my brother and I put ourselves on the bus willingly that Saturday morning. During the week, buses are yellow hearses and kids are the dead, but during the holy two-day hibernation, school buses are shotgun palaces of imaginary underaged driving and adventure.

By the way, you know why they're yellow? Because "lateral peripheral vision for detecting yellow is 1.24 times greater than for red." In other words, school buses were very close to being the color of spilled blood.

No one is surprised by this.

I don't remember what games Joe and I were playing on the bus, but I'm guessing Joe was pretending to drive and I was begging to pretend to drive. I'm guessing he was saying "No," so I was threatening to tell Mom.

"Go ahead," he said, but I wasn't doing that, and he knew it. How often in childhood do you get a sleeping school bus of your own? I wasn't going *anywhere*.

Suddenly, the big back door of the bus made a sound.

We turned in time to see the door swinging open, slowly. Inch by inch, it revealed someone we didn't recognize.

Because buses are tall and people are the height of people, all we saw once the door opened all the way was a stranger's head, which reminds me of a decapitation story I know.

My other grandfather, Edgar, told a scary story from his childhood. At around five or six, he was mingling with railroad workers down at the tracks one day. A man tapped him on the shoulder and said, "Wanna see something?"

"I am a child," said Edgar. "I want to see *everything*."

He followed the man to the side of the tracks. There sat a basket. It was covered with a red rag.

The man lifted the rag. "See?" he said.

Edgar leaned forward and looked in. He saw a roundish thing with brown hair on top. Ears on the sides. On the front of it, a face. He put it all together and realized he was looking at a severed human head in a basket.

I don't know what his reaction was, and I don't know what the peep-show man did or said after showing him, though maybe he said, "And *that*, my young friend, is why you gotta be careful around the tracks. Now go home, play, be happy, and try to have a nice, dreamless sleep tonight."

Though I agree that safety is important, not every completely effective teaching method is the best.

In my story, the head was still attached, connected to a man, and it spoke: "Hello, boys."

We returned his "Hello" then strolled to the back of the bus to see if this stranger was dangerous; with strangers, you never know until they're trying to murder you or not. You have to investigate.

On the way, an odd idea entered my head. I don't know if it was my idea or if Joe whispered it to me as we approached the stranger, but I do remember thinking that if I did what I had in mind, Joe would love it. He'd think I was hilarious.

Back then, if you could make someone laugh, you had the right, for a brief time, to love yourself.

Nothing has changed.

Joe and I reached the back of the bus and looked down at the man. The man smiled. Then he mystified us by saying, "I'm your first cousin once removed."

We puzzled over the term "once removed," wondering if it meant he'd been once removed from society and sent far away but now was back early after good behavior or an escape.

Next, the man said, "I remember you guys when you were babies."

We couldn't argue against this because we couldn't remember those times and only half believed in them. But family's important, and you're supposed to talk to family when they talk to you, so we said, "Did you know school buses were almost the color of blood?"

He laughed. We thought of him as a friend. Joe invited him to play with us even though the guy wasn't a kid anymore. He thanked Joe for the invitation, then said he was actually here to tell us it was time to come inside for a doughnut break.

And we would have gone inside for a doughnut break if not for the crazy idea in my head, an idea that became more than an idea when I turned it into action.

Here's what I did:

I breathed in…

I leaned down…

And I spit in the face of my once removed cousin.

If I'd been one of those spitting snakes, the cousin would have gone blind, then Mom would have cut my head off with a shovel and made me into boots.

After spitting, my memory jumps ahead, skipping over important details: What did the cousin say after I spit on him? What did he do? Did he turn red and yell? Did he become a dangerous stranger? Did he lunge, trying to grab me and drag me off the bus?

And most importantly, was Joe laughing?

When my memory cuts back in, I see Mom. She must have lunged and grabbed me because now she's dragging me across the driveway by the wrist. I am crying. We're heading for the car. For home. This is part of why I'm crying, because the visit is ending early. No doughnuts. I might never see doughnuts again.

All I'm going to see is a speedy car ride home then punishment of some kind. The kind? Who could say? I'd never spit in a relative's face before.

If, on the way home, I'd wailed, "What are you going to do, Mom? What are you going to DO?" Mom might have said, "I don't know," and she would have been telling the truth. It takes peace and hours to invent a punishment that fits the crime when the crime is unheard of and horrible, and Mom would have been too angry in the moment to invent and then explain.

And now that I'm a parent, I realize she was probably embarrassed too. People assume a child's evil is mostly put there by the parents, which means my spit had given everyone what they assumed was a glimpse into the inner workings of our home, a place where we learned from Mom and Dad how to disrespect one another by voiding bodily fluids into each other's faces to begin or to win arguments.

I don't remember my punishment, but I do know I never saw my cousin again. This time, he'd been removed for good, and it was my fault.

I feel shame when I think back on that day, shame and bewilderment. What kind of kid does what I did? And what else is he capable of? If the idea had been, "Kick the stranger's nose bone up into his brain," would I have done it? And would the reason have been the same, to make Joe laugh? *Would* he have laughed? And if he had, would I have felt no guilt for murder?

As ashamed as I feel, if I hadn't spit in my cousin's face, I wouldn't remember that day at all. It would have slipped through my memory's fingers without even leaving a stain. That beautiful summer Saturday, the fortifying prospect of doughnuts, the rare thrill of a whole school bus to ourselves... all of it gone. Lost. A loss that would shear from the length of my life a marvelous afternoon, and so much more than that: because time in childhood, according to child science, is fifty times longer, wider, and deeper than the times that follow after. Therefore, ninety percent of life happens in childhood. Adulthood begins the moment you round the bend and see the finish line in the very near distance. Lose time in childhood, and your life grows so short you begin to wonder if you ever lived at all.

So, if I could, would I take back my spit? Would I shake the cousin's hand instead of temporarily blinding him? Would I listen to the terrible idea in my stupid head, call it terribly stupid, and then keep it to myself?

No.

I would not.

I could not take it back. Because I've always believed it's good to live as long as I can.

And I have a feeling the cousin wouldn't *want* me to take my spit back. He remembers that day. He has to. Without the spit, though, he wouldn't. He'd lose the day, and that would be a tragedy, because he's at an age by now where he can't afford to lose even the smallest scrap of time. Losing that afternoon might throw off the balance of his life and send him tipping into the grave.

I like to imagine that if we saw each other today he'd say, "Thank you." He might hawk up a question: "Remember me?" And I'd say, "Always. And I always will." Then the cousin would spit in my face, returning the favor, giving me something else to remember him by.

A great gift.

A way to remember a moment, a day, one that otherwise would be half erased in two days and gone almost completely by the weekend.

I'd wipe the spit from my eyes and say, "Thank *you*," though I'd have to raise my voice over the sound of laughter.

Joe's laughter.

He'd be there too, of course. Laughing and high fiving the cousin, grateful for the memory.

But for the laugh, he'd be over the moon.

your doodles, memories, illustrations, story ideas...

## LESSON 6:

# The More You Love *Star Wars*, The More They Can Hurt You

First grade.

Harry and I were swinging on the swings, swinging and jumping off at the highest point, which means we were flying and falling, slamming the ground with our rubbery, first-grade bodies, then doing it again, all while discussing *Star Wars*.

I was explaining what *Star Wars* meant to me:

"I love it more than anything," I said.

"More than God?" said Harry.

"What? No one can love *Star Wars* more than God does."

"No, I mean do you love *Star Wars* more than you love God?"

"God invented stars and war," I said, "so loving *Star Wars* is like loving *him*, which he requires. In other words, I will not be entrapped by you, Harry."

I didn't say this, of course. I was too young. I thought it up years later, in adulthood, which is the point of adulthood. It's that zone of relative strength from which we journey back into the caverns of childhood, showing up like big, bad brothers of our younger selves, born to fight for the family, and we conquer.

Anyway, my buddy and I swung on the swings, talked *Star Wars*, and we did other things kids did in those days. For example: When two swing-set kids caught each other's swing rhythm in 1987 and their swings aligned, they hollered at each other, "Get out of my bathtub!" whatever that means. I didn't know what it meant then, and I don't know now. But I loved it, and I love it.

Harry and I got into each other's bathtubs then got out again in the best way to get out of anything: We jumped out. We flew.

We hit that New England granite-packed ground and bounced. The slam knocked an old-timey "oof!" out of me, which I chased with a laugh. Harry's slam knocked something out of him too:

It knocked the impossible out of him, which I chased with some impossible of my own, and he chased *that* with a miracle. You'll see what I mean.

Here we go:

Harry hit the ground then said, "You know Han Solo's gun?"

I said, "The DL-44 heavy blaster pistol manufactured by BlasTech Industries during the Galactic Republic years? *Know* it? When I die, though I don't believe in death—"

"Me neither," said Harry.

I grinned. "What's death?"

We laughed at death.

"When I die," I said, "I'm getting a DL-44 in heaven."

"So, you know it?" said Harry.

"I was *born* knowing it. Everything else I've had to learn the hard way: by learning."

"Well," said Harry, "I have one. I have a blaster pistol. I have Han Solo's real blaster pistol gun."

"You have *WHAT?!*" I shouted.

While I was paralyzed by shock, he ran back to his swing, swung again, jumped again, and flew, and while he flew, he said, "I have Han Solo's gun. It's not something fake or untrue or anything like that. When I say I have it, I'm making a true statement. Believe me. I have it with me back in the classroom."

This is when I performed the impossible thing I mentioned earlier:

I completely believed him.

But this feat of mine was effortless. When you're six, it's incredibly easy to believe a flying boy.

Harry landed. With grace, he struck granite, bounced, rolled, then stood up and said, "It is clear from your shock paralysis that you believe me. If what I said wasn't true, I'd be faced with a choice right now: To tell the truth or commit to the lie out of fear or possibly a perverse desire to further manipulate and harm another human being. But, since what I said about the blaster *is* true, you have nothing to worry about."

After that, it was time for the miracle.

Harry said, "You can have the blaster if you want."

My soul uttered a sound. The sound of a long-lost key turning in a long-lost lock. Within its treasure chest lay all longings fulfilled, all questions answered, all cares and terrors washed away, leaving behind a heart burning with happy idolatry.

It goes without saying that I became as alive as 50 living boys. Naturally, I gained abilities. I flicked my eyes to the school's bell. It rang. I flicked hot blood into my shock-frozen body, breaking the shock. I ran. Harry joined me, and we raced for the first-grade classroom, raced for his cubby, for my DL-44.

"Dear God, the Lord," I whispered, "I love you so much more than I love free blasters that are real, so I'm not going to hell, okay?"

God spoke: "If you love me so much, why have I never seen you run toward church with so much speed, excitement, and belief?"

"Because," I said, aided by myself from the future, "church isn't God."

"Good," said God. "You've learned everything you need to know. I can take you to heaven now if you like."

"Actually, I'm good. I'll just wait for heart disease like everyone else, if that's all right by you."

"Done."

I remember perfectly what was going through my head on the way to the classroom: I imagined taking my blaster into the woods and blasting trees. I'd done similar things with a machete. I downed an entire young-growth forest of poplars. Dad knew it was me because all the stumps were about the height of a first grader with a machete. But if I knocked down forests with a blaster, no one would know it was me, because who on Earth but Harry and me would ever believe blasters are real?

As I ran and dreamed, I laughed. Harry laughed with me. And when I heard Harry's laugh and saw the kindly shine in his eyes, I learned a great truth: Life is extremely good when you live it all by yourself, but it's better with people. They tell you truths, they give you gifts, and they keep you from laughing alone.

We reached Harry's cubby. It was full of papers, broken pencils, markers as dead as dry bones, a single Velcro shoe, a few G.I. Joe pelvises, and through it all, Harry dug and dug, and I believed and believed in my prize, and I had visions.

I saw the trees that would be my first bloods, the pines on my front lawn that made my hands sticky. Pitch trees. I couldn't stop touching them, those sticky perverts. I imagined slicing them with laser fire, leaving behind stumps smoking with remorse. And the forests primeval would watch and tremble.

Harry, digging and digging deep, suddenly stopped. "Oh no!" he said. Then he said, "Crap!"

But I was dreaming too hard to understand his words. I misunderstood them. I thought his "oh no!" meant, "oh no! I'm about to give away the greatest reason to live I have ever had," and his "Crap!" meant, "Will my best friend, Dan, even need best friends for a decade or so while he lives in a laser-induced state of high functioning joy-madness?"

Harry went back to digging, wildly now, and I watched him dig, seeing exactly what he saw—nothing. Still, I hoped. I was so deep in hope, my gut had gathered up all my dreams and visions and compressed them into something better than pearls and diamonds. I grew in my belly a hunk of faith so blind it didn't care at all about what it failed to see in that cubby.

Because the blaster was there.

It had to be.

"Shoot." Harry stopped digging again. "I think I... I think I maybe lost it."

Now my belly grew something else: a spider with freezing feet. It reached up and plucked one of my heart strings, yanked it back like a bow string and shot an arrow of doubt up into my brain's pristine, tender, and trusting underbelly.

I tried to speak, to say, "You, Harry, are mistaken," but all that came out was a gasp that smelled like a deflating soul.

Finally, I managed: "Lost?"

"Yeah," he said. "IT WAS RIGHT HERE!!! Dang it!"

The trees of Maine breathed a sigh that smelled like oxygenated relief. My heart went molten in a blink then cooled to a lump of bone in another blink and fell into my gut, landing as heavily as fifty dead boys, sending dream shrapnel upward, strafing the brain's underbelly so hard it cut through to the jaded overbelly. My body spasmed. Every muscle tightened, locking me in place so fast and violently they cut off a portion of my memory right there, leaving a bit of me trapped in that moment forever.

I am 6 years old.

I am staring into a cubby full of trash.

I am hit so hard by doubt that though I still believe I'm getting my blaster, I only 98 percent believe it.

"KEEP DIGGING!" cries the 98. "It has to be there! It *has* to!"

And this might explain why today I am a person cursed with hope. Because in my deeps, there's a six-year-old boy locked in a memory cut off before its bitter conclusion.

That boy is still a believer.

Only 2 percent of him feels deception's sting. Only 2 percent of him has learned how to manage his expectations and never fully trust anyone again. The rest of him, the majority, believes his dream come true is buried only a few pencils and pages away.

He's that close.

*I* am that close, forever.

So, I go back. I visit that memory that has no ending yet, which means it's a cubby full of possibility. I visit. I stand beside myself, big bad brother to myself, and I say, "Don't give up, Harry." Never give up, my friend. Dig and dig some more, because you, me, and I know what we all know:

Our dream is true.
Our dream is close.
It simply *has to* be there. So, keep digging.

## LESSON 7:

# If You Want Your Parents' Attention, Run Over Something They Love

For a brief and shining time, I was greater than my brother, Joe.

Before this, and directly after it, I lived the life of Dan the Younger, Dan the Inadequate:

When I drew, Joe showed me his superior drawing and said, "You can't draw." When I tried to be tall, he was taller.

So, I tried speed, he was faster. Strength? No contest. When I tried to out-eat, out-think, out-funny him, he called me "Fat Boy," "stupid," and "annoying."

But don't you dare feel bad for me. I wasn't helpless.

I had violence.

For example, one time after being tormented by Joe, I threw a small log at his head. Unbelievably, it hit his head. I'd wanted it to. I'd aimed it as well as I could and given it the necessary speed, but it was still unbelievable. In those days, I had absolutely wild aim. Sometimes it was perfect, and sometimes the things I threw with all my might went behind me instead of in front.

My direct hit was also hard to believe in because it happened in a moment of rage madness, one that ended as soon as the log struck. My rage broke, and I looked back on my attack through the eyes of a different boy, an innocent boy, not the log-throwing type at all.

But there I was, my arm still following through, and there Joe was, screaming, and there Dad was, because he'd seen it all.

What happened next gets a little "out of body" in my memory. I see Dad throwing me onto the ground. I see him picking up a much bigger log than the one I'd thrown at Joe. I see Dad as a silhouette standing against the sky, standing as tall as Moses in a tablet-smashing mood. And then I see the log coming down and slamming the ground beside my head, making a thump I can feel in the tips of the roots of my teeth.

I've always known what Dad's log lesson meant: When you harm others, harm comes to you.

But now I wonder. Maybe it wasn't a lesson so much as his own display of rage madness. If that's the case, I'm lucky Dad's sanity returned *before* the throw instead of after it, like mine had done.

Anyway, my moment of greatness, when Dan The Younger became Dan The Superior, was made possible by an operation Dad performed on Joe's bike: He removed the training wheels. This reintroduced an instability Joe hadn't felt in years.

I had no idea why Dad didn't operate on my bike, but I said nothing. Never draw the attention of a forgetful executioner.

After the amputation of Joe's extra wheels, I couldn't believe the drop in his skill level. He tipped over. He fell. He fell again. And when he didn't fall, his front wheel waved back and forth like a polygraph needle. The truth? I was better. I dominated the competition overnight, and I said to Joe a glorious thing: "You can't ride. I can. See? Watch me go." I said it over and over as I raced circles around him, my training-wheel wingmen catching me, daring me to circle faster, circle tighter, until I was so close to Joe I could whisper and be heard:

"I'm Fat Boy, huh? Stupid? Annoying? Maybe so, but you can't bike, and *I can*."

I leaned left, leaned right, I tempted Fate then I spanked Fate, which made me let out a war whoop while riding with no hands, no feet, no eyes. My pride glowed like atomic waste. But in my happiness and satisfaction, I got a little lost, and whenever that happens, I tend to do evil things.

I did two evil things.

## Evil Thing Number One

Because gravity couldn't hurt me, in other words, because I was beyond natural law, I left moral law behind too and entered the realm of animal thought.

Animals can surprise you. You'll do a great job training your bear to get photographed with random families vacationing at your circus, and your bear will play ball for years, until one day, she grabs a whole family and kills it.

What happened?

A compulsion entered your bear's brain. A thought neither bad nor good as far as the bear was concerned, even though it was breathtakingly violent. With bears and other beasts, morality isn't even in the building. The bear's thought was as innocent as any other bear thought. Like *I stand here. I obey. I don't kill this whole family. Wait, yeah, now I'm killing them.*

My animalistic thought, which automatically became my action (that's how animal thought works), played out like this:

I was speeding around in the driveway, watching Dad as he helped Joe balance, watching Dad jog along beside him, watching Dad encourage him, laugh with him, love him, then I aimed my bike at Joe's, raced toward it torpedo-like, and smashed into it.

Down he went.

I howled with joy. Joe raged. Dad flabbergasted. And though he didn't throw a log, I remember him yelling. I remember his question: "Why did you *do* that?!"

It is the question of all parents.

And the answer of so many children, an answer parents don't like, was my answer that day:

"I don't know."

I didn't. I still don't. It was a moment of raw bear brain.

"Well, you're going to have to do better than that."

A confusing thing for Dad to say, because he was the one always teaching me there's nothing better than the truth. I was stuck. All I had was the truth, which was, "I don't know why I did it," but Dad wanted something better.

Maybe all he wanted was a boy, not an animal-brained lunatic, even though this animal of a boy was a god on four wheels.

## Evil Thing Number Two

Everyone was in the driveway: Joe, Dad, Mom, my baby sister Meg, and me.

Meg was toddling around on her 1-year-old legs, trying and falling and falling again. She and Joe were a lot alike. I'd never been happier. *Joe has become helpless like babies.* I wove infinity symbols around the family, especially Joe. I rode faster, faster, sideways, backwards, never falling, not even close.

Yet no one noticed.

Mom helped Meg walk. Dad helped Joe ride.

And who but the martyred saints, angels, and Holy God himself cared that *I* could walk and ride without any parents at all? Parents would have only slowed me down. But maybe I wouldn't have minded. Maybe all I really wanted was for them to notice and acknowledge that I was more than a beast on a bike, more than a boy who rendered Joe meaningless.

I was art.

Living, rolling art.

In that driveway, however, I was invisible art. Which is possibly why, when I did what I did next, no one tried to stop me.

I carved my infinity loops, trapping the whole family inside them, trapping Joe. Suddenly, Mom allowed Meg to walk a greater distance on her own. Meg crossed the driveway. Everything with her walk was in working order: right leg, left leg, right leg, left. Arms up and out for balance like a zombie. Happy face, a giggle, and a full heart.

Then, she fell.

Face first into the driveway dirt.

And directly into my path.

In that instant, the animal brain returned, and I received an idea. It wasn't complicated. Maybe it wasn't innocent. Whatever it was, it was this:

My brain said, *Jump her.*

Without a word of protest from the civilized side of my mind, I peddled toward Meg's prone and screaming body as fast as I could.

Mom and Dad still didn't see me. I have a feeling they only had eyes for Meg in that moment, but if they did see me, they likely thought I was racing to my little sister's aid: *Look, it's another one of our children. Where's that one been this whole time? I'd forgotten what a good boy he is, and so good at drawing if you recall. Look how tall and fast and strong he looks. And his biking? Magnificent! But isn't he just the best of all when it comes to helping clumsy, bumbling babies in need? Look at him go!*

And I did go. Like a rocket. Like a rocket that can't tip over and is aiming for the center of a big mistake.

I had the driveway's downslope to boost my speed, which was already incredible, so when my parents realized I wasn't rushing to help, there was no time to step in.

No time to stop me.

All they could do was watch.

I neared.

Mom and Dad gasped.

I held my breath, pinning it behind a grinding smile.

I neared even more, and then...

I struck her.

I jumped her.

Now don't you dare make the mistake of thinking I jumped *over* her in a bunny hop.

No way.

I used her body as a ramp. I hit her with my front tire, striking then pulling up at the correct split second, which saved me from flying over the handlebars. In case you didn't know, this takes incredible skill. Next, the back tire and training wheels hit then bounced upward, bouncing their bike and boy upward too, and while Meg screamed, I got air.

It was impressive air considering how bad bodies are at being bike jumps.

And it was precarious air. I got a little twisted and landed poorly. But like I said, it didn't matter how I rode my bike, well or poorly. With my training wheels, I couldn't crash.

Therefore, I didn't crash. But Mom did scream, and Dad did yell. And while Mom headed Meg's way, Dad headed my way with a will and with all the justice he could carry.

The executioner had remembered me after all.

Joe, who was biking as badly as ever, watched wrath envelop Dan The Younger. Dan the Doomed. He watched so carefully he fell over, smiling all the way down.

And though my punishment was possibly severe at suppressed-memory levels, which are the next levels up from the log-level, for the first time that day, maybe the first time in my life, I, a rare piece of athletic bear-headed art, was the only thing on everybody's mind.

Hallelujah.

Just one jump of a sister, and I became Dan the Seen, Dan the Heard, Dan the number one hell-hot focus of his family's attentions.

How do you like me now, Joe?

# LESSON 8:

# Your Balls are Just Balls, But Gremlins are Forever

I went over to Brian's house to play computer games, and we both sat there watching Brian play.
 And only Brian.
 "Can I play?" I said.
 "In a minute," said he. "Watch this."
 I watched it. I watched it for 10 more minutes.
 "Can I play *now*?"

"Hold up, I just want to do one more thing."

He did 24 more things.

Thank goodness for Brian's mother who loved justice. Her name was Ann. I knew this because Brian called her "Ann" instead of "Mom," which I think means Brian was a low-functioning sociopath who sucked at sharing. Ann happened to be passing the computer room and recognized immediately what was happening to me.

She stopped in the doorway. "Brian, let your friend play."

"In a minute."

"No." Ann snapped her fingers. "*Now*."

"Fine."

Unfortunately, Brian didn't move.

He played on.

I had a feeling he knew Ann was still standing in the doorway, then in the room, then right behind him, steaming the top of his head with her nostrils, but he pretended not to know, just like he'd pretended not to know a human being burdened with huge and significant computer needs and feelings was sitting right beside him for hours, a valued guest who had been manfully wasting youth away in the dead end of this friendship.

He kept playing, even muttering to himself the way a person will when playing computer games all alone, for example: "This game is *fun*. And though I am not a likeable kid, which is why I have only one friend, I'm never sharing the good things I have, though sharing would help the survival of my one friendship, a friendship that doesn't seem to benefit my wonderful friend in any way, and yet somehow, he hangs on. Wait, I know how: He hangs on by the magnificent tensile strength of his moral fibers—"

Ann cut off this muttering with a sigh and a spicy "*Brian*."

Though I, like Ann, loved justice, I hated what was happening. It's terrible being at a friend's house when their parents are parenting right in front of you. Like you're not even there. In a way it's nice, because it shows they trust you not to report them to child services, but it's also very uncomfortable, and it can be scary. It's like getting between a mother bear and the cub she's fixing to eat.

Though Ann had said "*Brian*" spicily, he remained unmoved.

Therefore, she reached down for the power cord.

Stone-cold Ann.

"No!" Brian screamed. He jumped out of his chair so fast you'd think Ann had threatened to pull the plug on Brian himself.

He gave my shoulder a little shove. "*Your* turn."

"Go ahead," said Ann, slowly removing her hand from the cord.

In the double ugliness of their gaze, I crept into the player's chair. Then I played. Brian seethed on my left side. Ann seethed on my right. Even the best computer games are difficult to enjoy this way.

Thankfully, Ann left, though first she said, "Your friend gets *twenty minutes*. I'm watching the clock."

Brian acknowledged this by grinding his teeth to powder then blowing them out his nose in a mist of hate, which created a red rainbow by the light of the computer screen, and so forth.

I was happy. Twenty minutes is a childhood unit of time containing eternity. It is the early version of the grownups' unit of time called a "lifetime."

I don't remember the computer's game at all, but I imagine it involved a blocky little traveler who loved stomping other lifeforms to death for exercise, coin, and for the crown.

I played well. I did things in one try that had taken Brian two or three or twenty tries.

Friends are supposed to celebrate each other's victories, to cheer when their buddy is just generally more gifted and significant than they are, but Brian wasn't cheering.

Instead, every time I did something amazing, he punched the computer desk and spoke ironically: "You suck."

Still, I held nothing back. In my hands, the blocky traveler was unstoppable. Enemy flora and fauna were a joke. The bosses: jokes. Their sons and daughters? Practice. I leapt over pits that had swallowed Brian alive in their sleep and found secrets Brian never even dreamed of. I slaughtered my way up through the levels until the traveler's blood tide splashed at the feet of his thirsty, vampiric grandchildren, and through it all, Brian used his clap-incapable hands to beat up the desk, saying, "You suck, you suck, you suck!"

Suddenly, Ann called him into the other room.

He went.

I heard grim murmuring.

Mother and son were working their way through what my dad called a "teachable moment," and when Brian came back, he came back different.

- No more mean talk
- No more desk punching
- No more speaking or moving
- *At all*

I wasn't quite grateful. Brian had been a cock-a-doodle douche before, but now, in his stillness and silence, he was terrifying.

About six minutes into my turn, I arrived at a challenge Brian had called "the hardest part" and "the impossible part."

Brian stirred. He folded his arms, learned forward, and smiled big. "You'll never make it."

I made it.

I made it easily.

Then I went too far: I said, "*That* was the hardest part? Impossible? Dude, that was the easiest part and clearly possible," and I filtered all of this through a shiny, unsuspecting grin.

And that's exactly when Brian punched me squarely in my talented, incautious balls.

The pain was amazing.

Nut pain teaches you something you cannot know by looking at nuts: They are capable of pain far larger than their size. Their pain can't fit. It's forced to travel. It stomp-conquers the secret lands where you keep all the tender flesh of your core and all of your dreams.

I slipped out of the player's chair, poured out of it onto the floor, so I'd have room to writhe.

Brian jumped back into the player's chair, resumed play, and benefited from my progress.

And guess what?

I did not tell on him.

Had it been my brother or sister who punched my nuts, I would have force fed them to Satan if I could, but with Brian, not a word.

Why not? After all, I already knew Ann would fight for me. I'd be heard and believed, and action would be taken. Maybe she'd reset my twenty minutes. Maybe I'd be free to play the game for the rest of the visit while Brian was taken to a youth detention center.

But, if I told, there was also the possibility that the visit would be over.

When you tattle for something as meaningful as testicle attacks, sometimes you're escorted home immediately, and I could not afford to let that happen.

Not before supper.

At Brian's house, supper was chicken nuggets and French fries in the TV room, and it was the horror film *Gremlins*. It was heaven and a heaven forbidden by the laws of my house, which were obsessed with keeping all the tubes of my body and brain clean and unsatisfied.

By the light of the TV, Brian and I sat together on the couch, cheering for all the screaming and the death. Ann and her husband, Nelson, who Brian called "Nelson," smiled and laughed at us.

Anyone looking in on this scene would have labeled us a family.

A happy one.

And if they looked specifically at me and Brian, seated side-by-side, our mouths bristling with fries, our hands punching into the nugget bucket again and again as we roared together like brothers, they would have known they were looking at the very best of friends.

your doodles, memories, illustrations, story ideas...

# LESSON 9:

# You Can Steal Your Brother's Sin, But You Can't Steal His Glory

Fourth grade.
My brother slowly decomposed at his desk.
- He begged God for June.
- He did what we all did: dragged himself toward summer over the jagged cobblestones of time.

- He reached into his pocket for a pinch of teriyaki jerky dust to take the edge off, for he was a country kid, and all country kids carry dried meat of the hunt in their pockets, and that's when he found it:

Contraband.

His pocketknife.

Joe's heart pounded, hammered, thundered, etc., because bringing knives to school was against the rules.

It was only a matter of seconds before the other kids sensed or sniffed unauthorized pocket metal and tattled.

Seconds before a goose walked over the teacher's grave, whispering, "*Memento mori*, Donna. Also, that sweaty kid has a knife."

Joe imagined the bell ringing and pictured himself racing for the door with the other happy children, but then a voice would say, "*You.*"

He would stop, turn slowly in the doorframe, look back, and see the teacher, principal, guidance counselor, pastor, and cops.

**Next**: Joe getting blasted by hoses searching for other pocketknives and lice.

**Next**: Joe in juvie.

**Next**: Joe spending all his rec-yard minutes reading news articles about his world-famous younger brother, the joke-telling, monster-drawing, burp-belching Dan.

**Frontpage**: "EVERYTHING YOU ARE DYING TO KNOW ABOUT THE ONLY BOY AMERICA NEEDS!"

Suddenly, a kid in Joe's class sneezed, and Joe found himself standing, saying, "HELP!"

"Sit!" said the teacher. She said this because she'd brought a pocketknife to school too—every day—but hers was legal, and hers was in her head. It contained three blades (it had never needed a fourth):

- Blade One: "Sit!"
- Blade Two: "Work!"
- Blade Three: "*QUIET!*"

Joe sat.

He suffered from the weight of sin in his pocket, sin molded, stroked, and polished by the Swiss Army, a totally depraved force of soldier craftsmen interested in nothing if not the darkness of the pockets of children.

*What do I do?* Joe thought. *WHAT DO I DO?!*

Soon enough, he knew.

Every squeak of every desk and chair rhymed with the ugly word "confess."

The hissy knocks of chalk on the board said it too.

A kid tilted with skill, loosing a decently stealthy fart. Hidden within the purge was an eerie, aromatic message:

*Confessssssss.*

So, at recess, when the bell screamed, "Confess!" Joe confessed.

While his classmates galloped outside to swing, snack, and bully, he crept up to the big desk.

"*What?*" said the teacher.

Joe placed his knife and life on the big desk in a bed of lint and beef jerky dust. "I'm so sorry!" he said, eyes floating. "I forgot! I brought it by accident!"

The teacher looked at the knife. She looked at Joe. She shook her head but also smiled. "You're not in trouble, Joe. You did the right thing. Go out and play, and you can have your knife back after school."

Joe couldn't believe it. Had *he* been the teacher hearing this confession from some kid, from his younger brother, Dan, for example, he would have punished Dan to the fullest extent of the law, which possibly made him think, *The undeserved mercy I just received makes me long to be a better person, less cruel. For example, I really should treat Dan better, like an equal, or like he's a greater lifeform than me, which the evidence suggests—*

"Thank you!" Joe shouted merrily. He flew through the doorway, out of the school, and onto the playground to swing, snack, bully, and to thank God the teacher didn't seem to care at all about justice.

What happened next?

The usual for Joe: The goodness he'd just experienced did what goodness never does.

It continued.

The teacher was so impressed by Joe's confession she told Mom over the phone: "I'm so impressed by Joe's confession. Not many kids would do that. You raised a good boy. A smart boy. A great lifeform of a boy, the *greatest*."

That evening, Joe received additional honors:

- kind words from Mom and Dad
- kind grins
- so many hugs there weren't any left over for other nearby people
- and Mom and Dad spread words about Joe to my grandparents, prompting Grampa to point at Joe with a long workaholic's finger—an excessively knuckled scepter of blessing—yea, he pointed it at Joe and said, "Now *there's* a good boy. A *smart* boy. The only boy America needs!"

Somewhere in the background of all this celebrating, in one of the dark corners where younger brothers lurk, there lurked a younger brother.

His heart wrote a line of poetry:

"Any man's success diminishes me, / especially Joe's success—"

"What did you say, shadow child?" said the family. "What are you muttering in your corner?"

The boy glowed for a moment. His voice had been requested, called for. He answered: "Any man's success diminishes—"

But they didn't hear the rest. They were too busy screaming Joe's praises while bodysurfing him around the kitchen table forever.

In my corner, I muttered. I muttered additional true poetry, and I muttered a plan.

## The Plan

My plan was elegant in its simplicity, whatever that means, but I know this: It wasn't an exact copy of what Joe did. He had accidentally brought his knife to school and received honors. *I* would accidentally bring my knife to Sunday school and receive honors.

I sat in the little classroom on Sunday morning, sweating, waiting for my moment.

Joe had confessed one-on-one to the teacher and look what happened to him. Imagine what would happen to *me* when I, like a red-handed president, confessed before the masses.

*O, the pressure of the glory.*
*Let my life become a story.*
*May my win demolish Joe to death,*
*and may it be so gory.*

Each second passed like time bricks out of time kidneys, and I touched my pocket 900 times to make sure the knife was still there. It was. It was again. I looked like a kid under tremendous pressure. I looked like a kid touching himself 900 times. The teacher gave me the kind of looks you would expect.

"Do you need to use the bathroom, Dan?"

"Never."

*I need to be right here forever, for my moment is* nigh.

Class went on and on and I began to realize my moment was passing, which taught me there really is no right moment for the glory.

You have to seize the glory.

My spirit frothed and foamed with anticipation. *What if it doesn't go right? What if it goes* too *right, and they make me preach next Sunday?*

Suddenly, class was almost over. My heart pounded, boomed, and whatever.

I imagined missing my opportunity to confess; I'd get caught first, my sin revealed by the bulge in my pocket. I saw the future: Dan standing before the pastor, the deacons, the elders, the organist, and cops.

**Next**: Dan getting blasted by hoses searching for other bulges and lice.

**Next**: Dan in juvie.

**Next**: Dan spending all his rec time reading about the world-famous, joke-explaining, monster-denying, belch-suppressing Joe.

"THE ONLY BOY AMERICA NEEDS!"

Out of nowhere, a kid in my class sneezed, and I found myself standing.

"*Yes?*" said the teacher.

I reached into my pocket slowly, contritely, then I said something like, "What the... oh *NO!*"

I drew out my accidental knife in a natural way, the kind of naturalness only achieved by practicing so long in the bathroom mirror your mother says, "Are you okay in there, honey?"

"I will be. *I will be.*"

I said to my teacher and to the class, "I am so truly shocked and sorry. I accidentally forgot and brought this, my knife, to Sunday school by accident. What in the world should happen to me now that I'm not in trouble at all because I did the right thing?"

I tried hard to believe my teacher was pleasantly stunned by my confession. I studied her face for signs of stun, hoping for wide eyes, the shakes, and an open mouth murmur-spilling my praises. When it came to my fellow classmates, however,

I easily spotted their stunned condition, and more: They were stunned and sinning the fine sin of envy. They roasted in their envy. I could smell the jerky cooking in their pockets.

In this pause before my reward, I imagined my reward:

Mrs. Teacher would change the day's lesson on the shining dime of my example and say, "Now *here* is a child of God. A good boy. A *smart* boy. Unprompted, he handed over his secret sin. What about the rest of you and *your* secret sins? Would any of you dare to confess as this impressive young American has done?"

Silence from the children. And enduring shame. Oh, how they wished they'd brought their secret sins that day.

"I thought so," my teacher would say, then, "Stand, children. Hoist this boy high in the air and let us bodysurf him until he's had enough, which might be never, and that's going to be just fine by us. Now *cheer!*"

"Hurray!"

The children would lift me. I would rise on the sweet-and-sour surf of their jealousy. The teacher would say, "Chant with me: The only boy America needs! The only boy America needs!"

But before any of this could happen, the teacher looked from me to my knife then back to me and said, "Thanks for sharing? Put it away. Sit down."

No reward.

Stunned, I put my knife away. I sat. My face burned alive with embarrassment. I wallowed. I looked like a boy in a chair, nothing more. After all, that's all I was. Not a good boy, a smart boy. Nothing special. Just another child sitting in a plastic chair the color of humiliation, praying for death.

What was the Bible lesson that day? I don't know. I wasn't listening at all. Was it about Job? Probably. I see the flannelgraph Job slouching on his ash heap. His friends, happy to see him brought low, sit near him but so very far away. Their statements and silences say pretty much the same thing:

"You look like a guy on an ash heap, Job, nothing more. Because that's all you are now. Put away your hope and die. But first, we hear you have a brother."

"So?"

"We hear he's completely awesome."

"Oh."

"Before you die, would you introduce us?"

Job puts away his hope. He wiggles himself even lower in the ash, his butt making dents so deep they are ironically bottomless. He will never leave these shapely dents.

An hour or so after the disastrous class, I realized I was nothing like Job. *I* still had a reason to live: There was still a chance for a nice phone call from the teacher!

Back home from church, I was happy again, hopeful. I watched the clock and listened for the phone.

I imagined my teacher glowing from the confession she'd witnessed. She replays it in her mind as she paces back and forth, wiping her amazed eyes, shaking, joyfully ignoring her own children who keep asking, "What are these murmurs spilling from your mouth, Mother?"

She attempts to tell her family about me and my actions, but they don't understand. They are small people.

This makes Mrs. Teacher desperate to tell someone who will get it. She will *burst* if she doesn't find this intelligent person soon and tell!

*Of course!* she thinks suddenly. *Dan's mother! She will want to hear this. I would kill to hear something, anything, good about my own children. They are just so... oh, never mind. Anyway, I will call her right now!*

"Ring, ring."

"Hello, this is the mother of Dan speaking."

"Hello, this is the Sunday School teacher of Dan speaking. You are going to want to sit down for this one because it is such a great one."

"Is it incredible news about Dan?"

"It *is* incredible news about Dan. Merely thinking about what he did… it makes me feel like my own children are just so—"

"You do not need to say it."

"Thank you."

"But were you going to say that your own children are just so bitterly disappointing to you by comparison?"

"You are wise."

A companionable silence of understanding passes between the women, now friends, then my teacher transitions by laughing, "Ha ha ha, enough about me. I just wanted to tell you Dan accidentally brought his pocketknife to Sunday school today and turned it in even when he did not have to and could have just concealed it as a bulge in his pocket. Who doesn't have a bulge in their pocket these days? Anyway, has anyone in your family ever done anything like that before?"

"Not that I can recall."

"I didn't think so. Bottom line, Dan is a good boy and a smart boy. Are you going to have a little family party later including grandparents so you can honor Dan collectively?"

"Naturally," says Mother.

"What about your other son? Will he be there?"

"Who?"

"Your other son? You have two sons, do you not?"

"Oh, right. Slipped my mind."

"I understand. Pardon me for saying so, but it seems you do not need two sons when you have a Dan."

"Good point. I have never not thought of it that way before. In sum, who needs two when one already has the only boy America needs?"

And somewhere very nearby, a younger brother smiles so brightly his teeth light up the night of the dark corner where he has suffered for so long, but at last, his suffering is over.

His glory has begun.

your doodles, memories, illustrations, story ideas...

# LESSON 10:

# Occasionally, Violence Isn't the Way

In 7th grade, I walked into the gymnasium and witnessed two boys standing as close as salsa dancers and trying to punch each other in the face.

A fight.

I watched. I watched as hard as I could. My body reallocated sensory power, stealing from taste, touch, hearing, and smell, giving all to the eyes. I studied and memorized the path of every fist. I hoped for the best. I hoped to see a knockout and a harmless spell of unconsciousness, and though the boys tried so hard to give me what I wanted, they failed.

The atmosphere around their heads was a swarm of fists, but not one fist could connect. The boys were way too close. For kissing, that kind of closeness is key. But for punching a head, if you're that close, your fists get lost in the tangle of arms and can sometimes come out of the tangle in the wrong place and you punch your own head.

Desperate, one boy started kicking. This caught the other boy's attention. He tried kicking too. Unfortunately, the fighters couldn't connect with their feet any better than they could with their fists.

Then it happened.

The fight spontaneously ended.

It ended because the boys turned from each other and walked away. It was the most violent thing about their fight, this sudden stop, and they'd executed it perfectly.

I stood staring at the place where they'd been, trembling with disappointment. I'd invested time in this fight. I'd had expectations. Hope.

All for nothing.

You couldn't even call it a fight. So, what was it? Maybe it was a dance after all. A fierce dance of tremendous closeness and no touching whatsoever. Pretty impressive. I can hear the judges: "Gentlemen, you convinced us that you wanted to touch, *passionately*, and yet you achieved zero contact for close to three minutes. The physicality that takes? The training? It's staggering. Hats off to you both. That's a *10*."

In high school, I saw another fight. It happened in the locker room before gym class. Once again, I was investing time in a fight, developing expectations, growing hope. What was I hoping for in this fight? I wanted hooks, uppercuts, jabs, and haymakers. I wanted blood: bloody knuckles, noses, and ear holes, and I wanted piledrivers, chokeslams, rib breakers, and the spinning crucifix toss, whatever that is.

What I got, instead, was this:

One fighter, a gangly kid with lots of curly, grease-treated red hair, making him look like a wet Ronald McDonald in a Rob Zombie T-shirt, climbed onto the back of his opponent, a big kid with aviator-sized reading glasses and *Mad Max* style dental equipment in his mouth. Once Wet Ronald reached Max's summit, did he do what comes naturally? Did he pummel the top of Max's head with his elbows or stab his thumbs into Max's eyes? Did he jam a finger into the corner of Max's mouth and yank, giving him the classic Krav Maga fishhook? In other words, did he do what God made our bodies to do when pushed too far?

He did not.

With both hands, Wet Ronald pulled Max's hair. That's all he'd climbed up there to do. To pull and pull until Max cried out for mercy. Shrieked out. *Squealed*.

That was it.

The fight was over.

And these were the tough guys of my class. The ones everyone feared. The punks who could really mess you up if you crossed them, which now meant if you crossed them, you might find them on your back, their fingers braided into your hair, moves learned in nursery school, moves based on bodies filled with cartilage, not bones. Pitiful moves. Boring. Baby stuff. Never a tooth on the floor. Never a horizontal blood geyser from a broken eye socket. Just two bouncing babies yanking each other's scream strings.

That day, I wandered out of physical education educated and sad.

Where were the granite-cracking battlers, the big men, the cowboys? They'd gone the way of old soldiers: They'd faded away, though not before spawning a generation of

Maxes and Wet Ronalds, children rich in wrath, yes, but poor in showmanship.

*

My own fight occurred years before seventh grade and high school, and I must have forgotten about it while watching the latter-day fights. If I'd remembered it, I wouldn't have been such a harsh critic. I would have had compassion, maybe a comforting word: "After today, guys, when you're tempted to feel great shame over your performance, don't. Don't beat yourself up—you'd suck at that too. You're untrained, out of shape, and leaking grease. Not even Bruce Lee could make that combination look good. Bottom line, though you should never fight again, with anyone, it's possible that you're not a bad person."

My fight happened at Camp Calvary, a little Christian summer camp in the boondocks of Maine where my parents met. During Dad's time there, he was a motorcycle driving, short shorts filling, god of women. He loved that place. His Camp Calvary memories are some of the best he has.

So, when he sent me there, he probably thought I'd love it like he did. Or maybe he just hoped I would. I might have had hope too, but my hope ended on the first day while I waited in the registration line.

The line led to a shack that was only big enough to fit one registration person. I don't remember that person at all because I was only thinking about the kid I saw sitting in a kitchen chair on the shack's little porch. He was a skinny kid with wild brown hair. He was a kid wearing big, breezy red shorts and a huge smile. Believe it or not, he had an eyepatch. He was also a kid who was openly, masterfully, almost defiantly, playing with his testicles.

This was my introduction to Camp Calvary, a sign that my time there might not be as rewarding as my father's had been. And though Dad saw the kid who was unmissable, he didn't turn around and take me home. He must have decided the good of this place would outweigh anything traumatic that might happen to me and had already happened to me.

I found out later that Dad was right not to let the pirate boy scare us off. That kid wasn't the real problem with camp. If all I had to deal with that week was public self-entanglements, I would have had a great time. The real problem was everyone else. The mass of Christian kids, children who kept their hands off their balls when out in the open but were cold and cruel people. Everlasting life makes kids cocky. Grace is the fire-suit they wear with the collar popped as they burn bridges across the land. At Camp Calvary, kids stole from me, lied to me, bullied me, wouldn't let me therapeutically play tetherball alone, tried to force basketball on me, and not one of them warned me that when you eat five pieces of cherry pie after lasagna, you're going to die on a toilet in the middle of the night. I had to learn that the hard way.

One rainy afternoon, a friend and I were kicking a soccer ball back and forth in the gym, trying to look extremely occupied so no one would make us play basketball. It was going well. My buddy and I were actually having fun. So, we planned to hide in the bunker of our game and play it all week, right up to the second before diving into our parents' cars and locking the doors. No one can make you play basketball when you're locked in a car and yelling, "STEP ON IT, DAD! PEDAL TO THE METAL!"

Yes, our little two-man soccer game was great. But then, a new player arrived. He was a very little child, and unfortunately, he didn't come to play by the rules. He came to steal the ball from us. He kept appearing out of nowhere and kicking it away, forcing us to chase it down.

"Stop!" I said.

The kid didn't stop.

"Quit it!"

"*Never*," and he meant it. He raced in and kicked the ball away again.

My buddy looked afraid. I felt it too. With all this running around, chasing the ball, we were dangerously close to catching the attention of the basketball players, that whirling blob of shouts, squeaks, sweat, and no fun at the far end of the gym. At any moment, they might consider us available and reinstitute the draft. They would make us run back and forth, make us guard, make us remove our shirts. They'd scream things at us like "Foul!" "Double dribble!" and "Wrong team!" They would force us to sweat and collide with soaking, angry people on the court of unspoken rules for the rest of our lives.

I had to do something.

My buddy looked at me, pleading.

Invader kid kept attacking.

I made up my mind:

*This ends NOW.*

I chased the ball down, brought it back, and passed it to my buddy. He passed it to me. Back and forth while I waited for my moment.

I didn't have to wait long.

The little kid reappeared, whisked in, and booted the ball away again. This time, however, I didn't go after the ball.

I went after the kid.

To be fair to him, he was probably only bothering us to protect himself from basketball too. I should have realized this and had pity, inviting him to join our game. Then maybe others would have joined us too. It's extremely possible there were way more misérables at Camp Calvary than happy, thriving children. If we'd united, we would have become a gigantic circle of untouchables. If you tried to steal from us, lie to us, bully us, deny our tetherball rights; if you threatened our sleep with so much irresistible cherry pie; if you attempted to recruit even one of us for basketball, baseball, football, or capture the flag, you would have met the ball-kicking resistance of all of us.

Instead of sparking this revolution, however, I grabbed the little kid and put him in a headlock.

My plan had two parts.

One: headlock him.

Two: Twist the kid so hard his feet fly up, and while his feet are up in the air, release him. He'll crash land on the floor.

Results: This lesson will help him become a better person. After getting headlocked and thrown, he'll learn that actions have consequences. Most importantly, he'll learn that God is watching.

Part one worked. I achieved a successful headlock. I moved on to part two, twisting my body with great violence, which in turn twisted the kid. His feet uprooted from the floor as I had expected, sending his legs whipping out like kite tails in a hurricane, but only for a second, not long enough for me to let go. His feet, defying natural laws, came back down fast and re-rooted themselves to the floor. I had no choice but to try again. I gave him another fantastic twist. His legs flew out. But again, he shamed physics and returned his feet to the floor too fast for me to send him flying.

I had accidentally discovered the most unthrowable kid born in recent years. As untossable as Atlas, this kid, grounded as the World Turtle. It's like he'd spent his whole life in the arms of good people trying to headlock and chuck him; he'd become a master of thwarting this move of tough love.

Then one summer, his parents put him in a headlock and wrestled him into the car. They drove him to a summer camp and hurled him out the door. He landed on his feet, of course, but when he turned to leap back into the car, it was gone ("STEP ON IT, HONEY! PEDAL TO THE METAL!"), leaving the kid behind in a huge cloud of dust. Enraged, he looked for someone to hurt, preferably someone innocent and exceptional, for he believed the greater the victim, the greater the crime, and he was in the mood for committing great crimes. He searched and searched for this true gem of a human being. It wasn't easy. True gems at Camp Calvary were few and far between. But he didn't stop. His rage was bottomless, and it fueled his patience. Finally, mid-week, forced into the gymnasium by rain, he located his target: a young man kicking a ball as far away from basketball as one could get in that gym. Immediately, he attacked. And though his attack was relentless and heartless, he realized his exceptional target was unafraid. In fact, the child antagonist began to respect the target. Soon, his senseless attacks were motivated by self-hatred alone. The child wished he could put his own head in a headlock then twist and throw himself into a youth correctional facility. There, he would attack fellow inmates and guards until he was cast into solitary confinement. In his new cell, he'd have the time and silence he desired so greatly, the perfect solitude that would give him the peace required for writing. He would write a letter every day, each letter an apology to that young man, the gem. Eventually the letters, after their endless apologies, would transition into gratitude: "I'd never terrorized someone like you before, someone truly amazing. Kicking that ball away from you was like kicking a work of art away from a genius right before he makes his final brushstroke. The shock to my heart, my soul, was so great that I can say, I've changed. From the bottom of my heart, *thank you*. Thank you for being you."

I wish I'd known all this back then. I might have had sympathy. I might have given up on flipping the kid earlier. But I didn't know, and I didn't have sympathy, so I tried to drop him about twenty-five more times.

Soon, I was drawing the attention of other kids in the gym. Even some of the basketballers glanced my way.

Disaster.

So, I gave up. Yes, because I couldn't afford to catch the basketballers' attention, but also, I was exhausted.

So, I set the kid's head free from my lock and let the rest of him go too.

I expected the kid to run away rubbing his neck and to take a very long walk on which he reevaluated his life and then abandoned the worldview that had earned for him so much painful justice. Instead, he didn't go anywhere. He stayed close to me. Close enough to kick my shins if he wanted to. He wanted to. He kicked my shins, and it hurt terribly. Shins are sensitive because a body's padding is unfair. What did the butt do to get so much? What did the shins do to get nothing? Oh, the pain.

Though the kid was hurting me, I did feel sorry for what I'd done. Beyond my first violent twist, I hadn't enjoyed twisting him. All my anger had vaporized. From then on, I was only trying to throw him to the floor because it was the best way I could think of for getting him out of that headlock. In a way, I was doing all of it mostly for him. To set him free.

He kicked my shins.

I said, "I'm sorry."

He said, "Shut up." He kicked again.

"Stop, please. I shouldn't have done that. *Please* stop?"

More kicking.

It didn't seem like it was ever going to stop. I'd become a hippo: never alone because of the parasite-hunting bird living on his back, but my parasite was a shin-kicking bird, born to kick. Forever kicking.

Just when I began replanning my future to include the parasite, my soccer buddy rescued me. He kicked the ball past my attacker. Immediately, the kid broke away from my shins and went after the ball.

I don't remember what happened next, but here's what happened:

The kid came back with the ball and started playing pass with my buddy. When I tried to join in, the kid said, "Not you." Feeling bad about what I'd done to him, I obeyed, standing on the fringes of their game, watching. It was a good game. No stealing. No bothering. Nothing utterly ruined by outside interference. Just good old fashioned ball kicking.

Incredible: The kid was capable of more than tearing a game apart. He was playing and playing well, with honor. It seemed my lesson had worked. I'd taught him to be a better person, one who now believed in and feared the danger waiting on the other side of delinquency and corruption, a danger named God. By the many twists of my headlock, I'd tightened loose screws, repairing the kid, turning him into a useful citizen of the gym, and maybe even one of Camp Calvary's few good eggs.

I watched them play. I was even having fun, enjoying the harmony I had created. I wondered who else might benefit from a good wrenching of the neck. At the very least, it was a move I could save for later. True, it didn't help very much in a fight, but it worked wonders when it came to teaching people how to live.

Just as I was about to try again to enter the game that was mine, hoping the child had forgiven me by now, I felt a rough tap on my shoulder, a tap that was soaking wet.

I turned.

A sweat-glowing teen stood before me with a basketball in his hand.

"Skins," he said.

And for the next several years of that afternoon, without food, sleep, or the merciful release of death, I thumped and squeaked and sweat-shined myself, achieving nothing all over that floor.

My achievement was elsewhere: It was at the far end of the gym. It was my buddy and my enemy, the child I'd redeemed, thriving within the safety of my game.

# LESSON 11:

# You Never Forget Your First F-Bomb

First grade. Late winter.

Our teachers made us bring two pairs of footwear: boots for outside recess, shoes for inside. That week, the sun broke winter's back, turning the playground into a slush swamp. On Friday, I somehow managed to soak one shoe and one boot, so at the end of the day, I climbed onto the bus wearing one of each.

Joe, who entered the bus with me, shook his head at my boot-and-shoe combo. "Stupid," he said.

I was about to say, "*You're* stupid," but a voice from the back of the bus stopped me: "Look at that kid. One shoe, one boot."

I don't know why this was such a spectacle, but suddenly the back of the bus swarmed with heads, all looking my way. *Massive* heads. The heads of 8$^{th}$ graders, people we called the "Big Kids" because they were kids at the same time as being the biggest people ever conceived.

People like Guy Bradstreet. No teeth. No problem. You don't need teeth when you own your own logging company.

People like Billy Miles. He was taller than every teacher, heavier than every two and a

half teachers. When Billy ran on the playground, flocks of children fled before him like sandpipers fleeing waves, and whenever he ran, he made a sound. Out of his mouth came the roar of an 18-wheeler shifting into higher and higher gears. I can still see and hear Billy as he ran from one end of the playground to the other, reaching gears that truckers can only dream of.

Another Big Kid was Jim Blake. Head the size of an executioner's chopping block. Pale blond hair, nearly white, and forever buzzed. The inhuman blue eyes of a Siberian Husky, eyes that could cut through a quarter mile of woods to locate the kill-zone of a running buck. A nose that could follow that buck's blood trail in the dark.

And, at long last, the most significant Big Kid of all:

Amy Skates.

She had long, curly black hair, and light brown eyes, the biggest, brightest eyes in all of Maine. A girl so beautiful while smoking cigarettes that I wrapped little sticks in paper and mime-smoked myself blind every weekend.

Amy Skates was the one who'd noticed my boot-and-shoe boldness and said, "Look at that kid. One shoe, one boot." Then she said something else, and she said it right to *me*: "Come back here." She motioned with her hand, made a serenade of the word "sit," then patted the vinyl seat beside her.

Mountains avalanched. Lakes froze then thawed. Nine hundred penguins made love. *I had been chosen*.

I ditched Joe, knowing he would have done the same for me, and headed for the back of the bus, territory of the Big Kids, a place as far from authority as you can get on a bus, a dim zone of risk and possibility. Rumor had it that in those seats, the Big Kids smoked, drank, tattooed each other with pen ink and tacks, did drugs, built bombs, blasphemed, and ran sexual experiments worthy of honorary doctorates in sex ed.

And I was invited to join them!

So, I did.

So, I sat.

Yea, I sat beside *the one*.

She was wearing a French sweater: black and white stripes. Jeans so tight they looked like a stone sculpture of jeans. Tan work boots, the only footwear heavy enough to anchor her beauty to the mortal world. Bracelets all the way up, they rattled against each other when she moved, a kindness, for if her loveliness revealed itself to you without warning, you would die. But take heart: You would die so happy and stay so happy the Devil would think God sent a saint to ruin hell.

Amy was smiling at me. I've never seen so many teeth again. The perfect, polished, tenderly weeded gravestones of the hottest angels. Her smile, her eyes, and all the rest raised the romantic bar in my heart to the cruel heights of high-altitude pulmonary edema: headache, nausea, vomiting, fatigue, insomnia, and no regrets.

Amy pointed at my boot and shoe. "Why so cool?"

Cooly, I shrugged. "I don't know."

"Well, it's cool," said she.

To sit beside Amy was wonderful, but to be called cool in addition was divine, an anointing by the High Priestess of Cool herself. I looked for Joe so I could watch envy kill him, but he was blocked by the seats. So, I planned my future. Tomorrow, I would wear one shoe and one slipper. The next day, one boot and one sandal. The next, a rollerblade and a bare foot. On my wedding day, I'd stand at the front of the church while Amy marched toward me with all her heart, her shining eyes flicking back and forth gratefully between my scuba flipper and astronaut boot.

For a sweet instant, it seemed Amy and I were alone on that bus, alone in all the world, dual captains of the "marriage of true minds" wedding bus, a bus bound for parts of the world where the sun never set on my will to gaze at true beauty, the countries of the heart, in other words, where nothing more than a first-grade education is necessary, making Amy's education excessive, like her loveliness.

Our status as Earth's only people, our Adam and Eve-ing, was interrupted, however, by Amy's friends, her tribe.

The Big Kids.

They made their presence known.

People like Paula Bicks, a red-haired, green-eyed farm girl with a shotgun blast of freckles on her face and a slug of tobacco in her lip. People like Debbie Harlo, a skeletal, raven-haired girl with no eyebrows and the ability to roll her eyes into her head and pretend to die. And Tommy Turner, a neckless boy-man with an open wound for a mouth, a creepily high-pitched laugh, and a chin so pronounced it looked like the dead head of the twin he consumed in utero trying to push through.

All these faces rose above the seats like werewolf moons to gaze upon Amy's child-groom.

Toothless Guy Bradstreet was there too of course, and Billy Miles, our singer of truck song: I heard him making the mighty soprano roar of the great trucks' compression release engine brakes, the "Jake brake" scream, and his giant head joined the others. Jim Blake appeared too, his dog eyes sifting through me, down to my fear, confirming what his nose already knew.

I remember Jim's face better than the others. It hung above the seat in front of me as big as a prize pumpkin carved to look like the end of my luck. He leaned so close. To look him in the eyes at that distance, I had to look at his dead-blue eyes one at a time, turning my head from one to the other. He was smiling. He was chewing something, the cud of his tobacco-and-deer-meat lunch, as he fashioned something to say. In the meantime, he stared at me.

"Okay, Jim," said Amy, rolling her eyes, "you can leave him alone now."

Jim ignored her, and this helped him speak. He said, "Hey, fuck you, kid. Cool shoes."

"Thanks," I said.

Of Jim's six words, I understood five. The one I didn't understand was a word I'd never encountered before, and I turned it over and over in my mind, wondering what it meant.

For some reason, Amy slapped the seat and hissed at Jim. "Don't *say* that!"

"Don't say what?" he asked, smiling. "Don't say *fuck*? Should I not say fuck? Is fuck bad? I'll stop for fuck's sake. Oops, sorry! *Fuck!*"

Though Amy did her best to defend me, for the rest of the ride home, all the Big Kids took turns saying the word, coughing it, whispering it to me around the edges of my seat, weaving it into their conversations seamlessly, so that sometimes Amy didn't even notice. But I noticed. I collected each occurrence, especially those that slipped out of Amy's mouth when she, now and then, forgot that I was there.

As I gathered up the strange word, I wondered what it meant. It sounded a little mean. And it looked mean coming out of Jim's mouth and the mouths of some of the others, but it wasn't completely unpleasant. Sometimes it made people laugh. Sometimes it looked lovely, as beautiful as Amy's smiling lips.

Before long, the bus stopped at my house. I said goodbye to Amy, and she branded my heart with the freezing fire of, "Bye, buddy."

"Bye," I said again.

Her friends said, "Bye, little fuck," and a great variety of similar things, giving me a huge fuck-bouquet to carry home.

As soon as Joe and I were off the bus and it was driving away, shifting up through the gears almost as loudly as Billy Miles, who always harmonized with the bus, Joe asked, "Why'd they want *you* back there?"

"I don't know."

"Tell me *everything*."

And I did. Almost everything. I needed time alone with my new word before I revealed it to Joe.

That weekend, I listened for it everywhere. The Jim and Billy word. The *Amy* word. I listened at home. No luck. I listened at church. I imagined the pastor's mouth twisting with that exciting, sour sound, and then releasing it throughout the sermon:

"Blessed are the meek, for they shall inherit the fucking earth."

But no one was saying it. I thought back to the bus ride and tried to come up with fuck's definition. I remembered the Big Kids used the word during friendly-sounding talk, but it sounded best, most at home, when used as an anger word, which was how they used it most. I decided "fuck" was hot sauce for a sentence. It added kick. It was a word that shouted even when you said it softly. And apparently it was a word parents and pastors didn't like using. So, it was a bad word very possibly, an excellent and impressive word most definitely.

But still, I didn't know what it meant.

All I could come up with was the image that started popping into my head whenever I thought of the word or whispered it. I pictured a cow. I don't know why. Maybe because most of the Big Kids were farm kids, and I figured if they knew a word that was foreign to me, it would be a farm word, a technical term, which could be translated for the layman into "barn," "egg," or "cow," etc.

> **BARN:** "Good morning, church. Next Saturday, we're having ourselves a good old-fashioned fuck raising."
>
> **EGG:** "This chicken here? Oh, she's good for about a fuck a day."
>
> **COW:** "How now, brown fuck?" Specifically, a black and white fuck. A Holstein. That's what I pictured.

I felt correct but confused. Why is a word that means "cow" a bad word?

No idea.

I moved on to my next problem: Why is a word that means "cow" an anger word? But this one, thanks to Grampa, I could answer. Whenever he got mad, usually while working on something, anything, in the barn, he would say, "stinkin' rotten *pig*!" or simply "pig!" or "swine!" He did this in the place of swearing. He did this all the time. So, it was easy to imagine Grampa breaking a tool or skinning a knuckle and shouting, "cow!" shouting it the way a farmer would, the technical way.

And the more I thought about it, the easier it was to imagine myself shouting it too.

\*

Sunday afternoon.

Joe and I took advantage of the warm weather and flew kites on the slushy front lawn. Our kites were as different as we were: Joe's was noble and American, resembling a bald eagle, while mine was an anarchistic moth, complete with the huge, terrifying eyes on the wings and a moth's love of chaos.

Joe got his kite as high as airplane traffic, turning it into nothing more than a brown, white, and bald speck against the blue. My kite, however, true to its nature, was sick in the head. It refused to catch and ride the winds. Instead, it struggled on purpose fifteen feet off the ground while I ran back and forth as hard as I could, trying to drag life into the big jerk of a moth.

"Come on!" I shouted. I called it the usuals: "stupid!" and "idiot!" I called it "swine!" "pig!" and "stinkin' rotten pig!" Also, I said, "schmuck!" "you suck!" and "I'll pluck your yuckin' eyes out!"

My kite responded by flapping its flabby skin even more, mocking me. I begged for God's help, and that's when the kite aimed its head downward and dove.

When it struck the ground, something hot and saucy filled my mouth. My bottom lip sucked in, pulling into lethal position like the hammer of a gun. My top teeth met my lip and bit down, a formation made perfectly for a certain sound, made for only two letters of the alphabet—V and F—a potent formation, like when a thumb and middle finger come together for a snap, or when a speeding neutron touches the nucleus of an atom, or when a wayward kite strikes the ground with an almighty, earth shattering…

### *"FUCK!"*

I said it.

I shouted it.

Screamed it.

And Joe let go of his kite. Off it flew, high and higher, farther and farther away, turning from a speck to a mite, to a mote, to a molecule heading for heaven, carrying a message:

*Dear God, you'll never guess what Dan just **SAID!***

After Joe's kite disappeared, he stared at me, his face deathly pale and so happy. His mouth resembled a capital O, but a grin tugged at the edges, eager to sharpen his mouth for its fun and rewarding mission: *Your mission, Mouth, is this: Tell Mom. If you die on the way and have only enough life in you to say one thing, you will not say "I love you," you will not say "Bury me with my possessions." You will tell her what Dan just said.*

He ran for the house.

In two shakes of a fuck's tail, I stood before Mom.

Joe had delivered all the information: the screamed profanity and the resulting loss of his kite, which meant I should buy him a new one or give him mine *and* buy him a new one.

Mom sat in her rocking chair, rocking slowly. I knew from Joe's bloodless face, and from Mom's cold eyes, that my farm language, for some reason, wasn't hot sauce.

It was poison.

But why was it poison? I still had no idea. Maybe context played a part. For example, I knew you could scream, "damn!" when driving by a dam, and everyone in the car would laugh and love you. But you couldn't say, "Damn good sermon, boss," to the pastor. Every time you did, there wasn't laughter and love waiting on the other side. Just punishment. So maybe you could only use the term fuck when you were a farmer, like the farm kids, or when you were on a farm or near one.

**DAN**: Hey, Mom, while we're driving by this farm pasture, check it out: What are those two fucks doing?

**MOM**: Which fucks?

**DAN**: *Those!* The fuck trying to climb onto the back of the other fuck.

**MOM**: I'll tell you when you're older.

Whatever the reason, the word was bad, and I was in trouble. But whose fault was it?

*Not mine.*

I feared Mom too much in the moment to even think of the Big Kids, to blame them, but later I did. Later, I pictured myself in the back of the bus where I stared down each kid, from the biggest to the even bigger, and gave them back their mean, mysterious word, right to their faces. And I thought of Amy. Yes, she'd tried to protect me, but how hard had she tried? After all, she'd said the word too. A *lot*. And why hadn't she at least explained to me that I had to be very careful when and where I used the word? *Amy, my love,* I thought, *why?*

"So," said Mom, "where did you hear it? I heard you rode at the back of the bus. Did you hear it there?"

I nodded, tears forming in my eyes.

"Do you know what it means?"

I nodded again, tears dripping from my eyes.

Mom stopped rocking. "What does it mean?"

I explained. I broke down and told her everything, from the beginning. I started with the irregular weather, these stupid warm days. It was the weather's fault the playground was mostly slush, the same slush that soaked my sneaker and boot. Also, it should be noted, I didn't call home, crying for a solution, did I? I solved the problem myself, hoping certain people would be proud of me. It was either cry for home, forcing you to come get me, or go with my boot-and-shoe move. And how was I supposed to know my ingenuity would earn me an invitation to the back of the bus and an audience with Amy who might be my girlfriend at this point since no one can say for sure, but the odds look good. Granted, she's a little rough around the edges, but she's also the Princess of Maine and perfect, what with her hair, teeth, and jeans, and her come-hither hand patting the vinyl, a gesture that could launch a thousand good boys into crime—

"I understand," said Mom, "but what does the word *mean*?"

Joe's breathing changed. It went from little puffs of happiness, puffs scratching their backs on the fangs of his smile, to silence, his breath held for the drama of my definition.

"Mom," I said. I sighed. "It just means cow."

"What?" she said.

"Cow, it means a black-and-white cow. That's all! I don't understand why that's so bad! No one does!" I wept. "I'm *sorry*!"

Then, out of nowhere, Mom started laughing. She rocked the chair back hard and laughed hard.

Joe and I looked at each other, deeply confused. Our eyes communicated at a new level. Our eyes said, *What the hell?*

But when Mom caught her breath, some seriousness came back to her face and voice. "It doesn't mean 'cow,'" she said. "It's a swearword." Then she gave me a nice hug. "Now go out and fly your kite. And don't sit at the back of the bus anymore, okay?"

For a moment, I didn't move. Neither did Joe.

We were still waiting for my punishment, and Joe said, "What about my kite? He made me lose it."

"*Go.*" Mom pointed at the door. "We'll figure that out later."

And away we went, shaken.

A child had done something wrong. A child had done something very wrong, gotten caught, and a child had received no consequences. Even more amazing than this, a child had done all this consequence free, and a mother had laughed.

But why?

Joe and I wondered over this as we walked in a haze of bewilderment back onto the front lawn.

Joe flew my kite. In half a minute, he got it horribly high. When I told him, "Good job," and added, "It's still my kite," he ignored me and said, "I just don't understand."

I knew exactly what he meant. If it didn't mean "cow," what *did* it mean?

He continued: "*Why* didn't you get punished?"

I shook my head slowly, and I meant it. "I don't know."

We puzzled in silence, eyes on the moth eyes in the sky. The what-the-hell moment we'd

shared earlier still had us in its grip. We were a temporary team, united by the unknown, we were one, even though he'd ratted me out. Even though he was stealing my kite right in front of me.

I reached for the string over and over, but Joe wouldn't let me have it. "It doesn't make

sense," he said. "It's one of the worst swears. If *I* said it, I'd lose *everything*." The kite found a patch of bad air and started to sway and drop. "It's just not fair."

"But what does it *mean*?" I said.

"It means *you* get away with everything—"

"No, I mean the *word*. What's it mean?"

He said nothing. His eyes went back and forth, signifying thought. He was obviously

rifling through his own definitions. Whatever he and I thought it meant, knowing that it didn't mean "cow" put us one step closer to the truth.

The kite pushed through the bad air, found wind, pulled the line tight again, and Joe smiled. "I know what it means."

"Tell me!" I shouted.

"You'll tell Mom."

"No, I won't." I would. Vengeance is sweet.

"Yeah, you will," he said. "But ask your new friends next time you see them. Tell me what *they* say it means, so I can see if they're right."

"You don't know what it means."

"Maybe, maybe not."

Of course he didn't know. If he did, he would have given me tasks to perform, torturous ways to earn the definition.

We watched the kite in silence. Some would call it a companionable silence. But with brothers, it's just another Christmas Truce amidst two worlds at war.

Still, it was peaceful. So much so, that Joe even gave me a turn flying my own kite. He handed me the spool, which carried within it the power of the kite's pull, the sobering weight of success.

"*Wow*," I said.

"I know," said Joe. "Don't mess it up."

I did not mess it up, and the reason was this: While I flew, I thought of Amy. I wondered where she was, what she was up to, and *who* she was up to it with. Best case scenario, she was not spending time with some farm kid, a big and handsome dirty mouthed man-boy—

No.

She was alone.

She was walking the slushy fields of her farm, making the fields look French in her French sweater, and passing by cows while thinking nothing evil. She climbed a newly thawed hill, bright green, and gazed up into the blue, losing herself there, dreaming of waiting years for love to grow old enough to find her.

Here's what she didn't see in the sky: a bald eagle flying free of its captor, dragging a kite string and spool behind it. Because that eagle had crashed landed headfirst in a swamp and burst into just and funny flames. Here's what she *did* see: In the center of blue infinity, she saw a kite flying impossibly high, a kite with eyes looking down. True, they were moth eyes, but they were loving, eyes for her alone.

She sighed. She smiled. She didn't know kites could fly that high. It was a little shocking.

"Holy fuck!" she said, and though I didn't know what she meant by that word, I knew one thing she didn't mean, and that was enough to help me make another educated guess, one of many in a long line that would one day lead me to the truth.

What did Amy mean? What was my new guess?

Amy meant something complicated, dangerous, and grownup, something you can occasionally find at the back of a bus, or on a warm winter's day, making it feel like spring. She meant something that shouted even when you said it softly, a bad thing, but in a good way, something excellent and impressive and sometimes even hilarious.

Something just for me.

your doodles, memories, illustrations, story ideas...

## LESSON 12:

# Parents Who Don't Force Musical Instruments on Their Children Deny Them the Profound Pleasure of Quitting

"We have a surprise for you," Mom and Dad say.

You're eight years old, so you think it's a new bike, or a tiger. You're overjoyed. You can ride either one. You put out your hands and close your eyes.

They place something in your hands, something metal and cold, or wooden and hollow. Whatever it is, it feels nothing like a bike, or tiger. You open your eyes and see a violin, a flute, a mandolin, or a bassoon. You've had worse surprises. Poison ivy in your eyes, for example. Or that week when all your farts turned to big consequences for your pants. But this surprise isn't like those. This one, you have a feeling, won't go away after a little while. This one might hang around for a long, long time.

Or maybe when you close your eyes and hold out your hands, your parents guide you into the garage where you see a piano brooding in the back of Dad's truck. This is worse than a violin, flute, mandolin, or bassoon, because those things fit in garbage cans—but pianos fit nowhere, and they last. The only things left after the apocalypse will be cockroaches, piles of teeth, and pianos.

"Surprise! You're going to learn to play piano!" They shout this while Dad's eyes shout something else: "Because of how much this thing cost me, you're going to play it or die trying."

You look at the instrument. You look at Mom; she's atomic with happiness. You don't have to look to know Dad's mad; he's changing the temperature of the room. He spent a lot, apparently, and you don't seem to know what money means. It means, "Jump up and down with excitement right now or die trying."

Mom's eyes say, "You're going to learn to play this and win the heart of the world with your beautiful music."

Dad's eyes say what his mouth says: "Well?"

"Thank you," you say.

Mom weeps. She imagines you happily winning the world's heart.

Dad doesn't see what happiness has to do with it. He sees Carnegie Hall. He dreams of lurking in the audience, gnashing his teeth with pride.

"Go ahead," they say. "Try it out."

You tap a couple keys, pluck a string, or blow in the oboe hole. Maybe you pounce your hands on the keys with violence and it's actually kind of fun, all that noise. But Mom looks worried and Dad's even madder, if possible.

It's possible.

"That's not a toy," he says.

*Perfect.* The most expensive thing you've ever owned, a thing that could buy a thousand toys, is not a toy.

It gets worse. Lessons. Mom and Dad pay a person to be as mad as Dad when you hardly practice. The teacher, who smells like cigarette gum and funeral flowers, has a whole house full of things that are not toys. You wonder why she teaches children anything if she hates them so much.

Mom and Dad buy a metronome. It wags its middle finger in your face. It's a torture device, a clock that never advances time. But neither does the real clock, not while you're practicing. How could only one minute and seven seconds have gone by? Mountains whittle to dust in the time you've been sitting here wondering why some pervert put so many keys or strings or holes in this stupid thing.

You play. You squeeze out notes like tears from a rock, and every note stabs Dad's dream in the eye. Mom's smile tightens.

You get older. You've memorized a few songs. They hold on like scars. "Für Elise," "The Entertainer," and that Charlie Brown song, which makes people so happy they blow coffee mist like coughing whales.

Though Mom claps and cries, Dad knows they don't play Charlie Brown at Carnegie Hall. He starts wondering again if you know how much your gift cost him. You do know. You've offered to pay him back 500 times. You've offered your soul to hell if you could come home from school to a house without an angry instrument waiting inside, daring you to touch it so it can scream insults and discouragements.

Mom is hopeful still. She talks about your style. She can't believe your incredible memory for all those notes you know. She has so much confidence, in fact, that one day, one amazing day, she says, "I have a surprise for you."

You are not hopeful.

You've lost much of your faith in surprises.

She goes on: "I think you're ready."

Dad is listening, but he doesn't figure out what's going on in time to stop it.

Mom says, "I think you're ready to decide for yourself. You're at a level now that's so impressive. So…" she says, smiling, confident, "you can keep playing if you want to, but *only* if you want to. It's up to you now. What do you think?"

Dad holds his breath, slowly turning purple, quickly turning even older. He cannot believe what just happened.

Neither can you. But Mom has done it. She cannot take it back.

You pretend to think but something takes over, an old dead dream. It resurrects and rises, cutting through your fake pondering, and you sing out with all your life, "I quit!"

Your shout makes the guitar strings hum with concern. The clarinet-metal ticks like it just swallowed a lump of fear. The piano's smile becomes a wince of worried teeth.

You are free. They are for sale.

You imagine some other kid receiving the honking, twanging, mother-plunking curse you have just cast off. The pain they'll feel. Years of joyless noise. But it's all for a higher purpose. It's all to sweeten the intoxicating air of freedom that comes when they too sing out with all their might a declaration as lovely as the most beautiful song ever played.

### "I QUIT!"

You look at Mom with tears of love in your eyes.

You look at Dad with tears of triumph.

It *was* a nice surprise after all.

your doodles, memories, illustrations, story ideas...

**LESSON 13:**

# Not Everyone Should Be Allowed to Draw Your Face

When my grandfather had people over to the house for a visit, people who didn't know him well, he'd ask permission to draw one of them.

He'd say he was something of an artist, a hobby artist, and that he didn't do landscapes or fruit bowls. Only portraits. Then he'd ask if he could draw the visitor, for some practice.

This was a surprising and possibly flattering request, or maybe it was just weird. Whatever it was, people often said yes.

He'd have them sit in profile then begin.

The subject or "sitter" would sit very still, vanity taking over as they strained to make their nobleness rise to the top. They'd advance their chin, or lengthen their neck, or bite down and push a twinkle into their eye.

Grampa would glare at his subject, glare at his work. His dead silence communicated his state of mind: that of an artist who pours every ounce of his existence into every attempt to capture the elegance and severe beauty of the reality of your face.

Minutes passed. More minutes. The longer he drew, the more the sitter believed they were about to look upon a reflection of their truest self:

A masterpiece.

Finally, Grampa's agonizing would be done, and he'd say something like, "I think we might be finished here… wait!" then he'd add one more thing, and maybe another thing, and then finally, he would present his work.

"Ready?" he'd say.

"Ready," the subject would say.

Then Grampa would turn the portrait around, revealing the following image: the profile of a bald person who looked exactly like an elderly baby, a person with a nose bent in such a way that it could drip snot (and did drip snot) directly onto their huge, extended, and greedy tongue.

The portrait *always* looked like this:

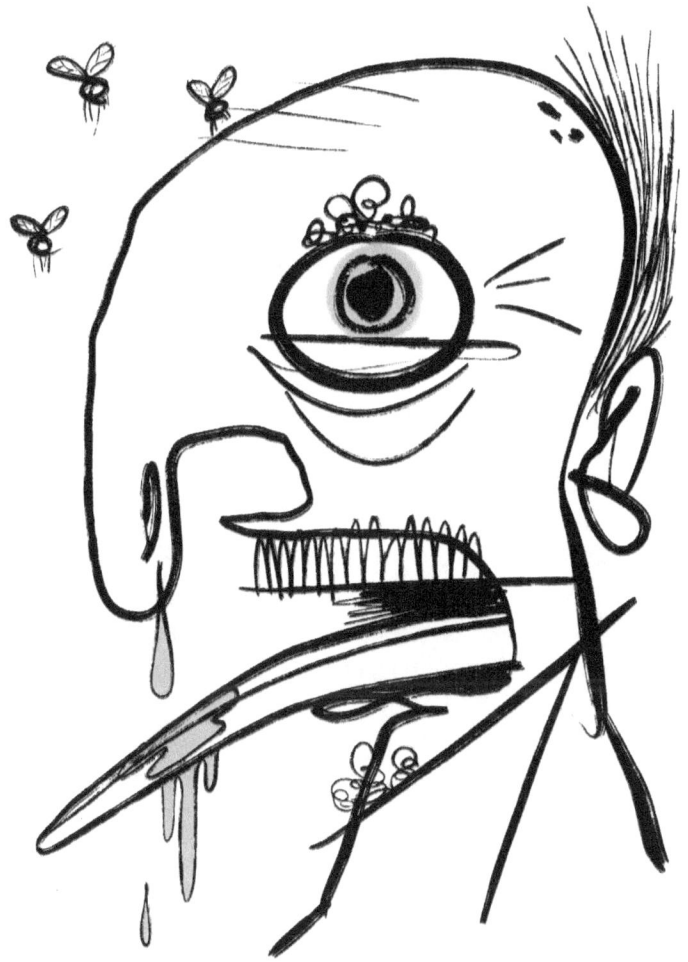

　While Grampa toyed with art, his youngest daughter took it seriously, turning herself into a real artist with real artist friends. One day, she brought one of these friends home from college for a visit.
　They were all having coffee when my aunt claimed her friend was one of the best illustrators she'd ever met. "She's drawn *hundreds* of portraits—"

"Probably closer to thousands," said the friend.

"What's your style again?" asked my aunt.

"I'd say realism, leaning toward impressionism, and now and then there's an expressionistic flair, but I can't predict it." Then she looked at Grampa. "I could attempt a depiction of you if you like."

He did like. He agreed.

The friend said he could sit any way he wanted as long as it was natural for him, and then she took out a vast drawing notebook from somewhere, many pencils too, and got to work.

Grampa sat in his natural way, with a finger hooked through his coffee cup, and an arm hooked over the back of his chair. Classic Grampa. I call the pose "The Cocky Lounging of a Wild Old Man."

My aunt's friend drew and drew, sketched and sketched, glaring at her sitter, glaring at her work, back and forth, and then she drew and sketched some more. She squinted her eyes, chewed on her tongue, grunted with dissatisfaction and satisfaction, held out her thumb to measure distance and proportion, she did everything you do when you're the best illustrator my aunt knows and you're drawing Grampa.

On and on she illustrated, the minutes ballooning into a quarter hour, then a half hour, and all the time, Grampa sat as still as stone, his chin strong, his neck long, his eyes twinkling with the excitement we all feel when we see reflecting in someone else's eyes the person we hope to be.

At last, the friend gave her work a final stare, twisted her mouth this way and that, sighed deeply, nodded her head, then declared the portrait finished.

"Wait!" She added one more thing, or two, then sighed deeply again. "Okay," she said, "are we ready to see?"

"I think we're ready," said Grampa.

The friend of my aunt turned the humongous sketchbook around and gave Grampa a look at himself, a *real* good look.

Filling the artist's page was the bald, elderly baby, the baby naturally lapping up a generous stream of its very own snot. The moment Grampa saw it, he roared with laughter. Believe it or not, he'd never guessed what was going on. He'd been tricked, caught somehow in his own trap, and best of all, he loved it.

He laughed gigantically.

All those years of drawing snot eaters had been building toward this master joke, a gift for him, a gift given by his daughter through a good friend.

Grampa held the drawing and laughed. He laughed until there were tears in his eyes, until there were snots in his nose, snots hanging above his gaping laugher's mouth, which opened again and again for more.

your doodles, memories, illustrations, story ideas...

# LESSON 14:

# There is a God on Frozen Ponds

If you're a child in Maine and it's winter, you either invent fun things to do outside or you catch cabin fever and emerge from it covered in your family's gore.

When I played outside with Meg, we played a hellish version of *Little House on the Prairie*. Picture two children crawling across the snowy lawn while pretending to have two broken legs apiece. A bear got us, or a drunk, an outlaw, a bull, boars, tip-over horses, a kicky mule, but mostly a kicky morphine addicted demon dabbling pastor's wife, and on top of everything else, there were always blizzards. Blizzards make finding your house impossible, especially if it's a little house dropped like a single tear into the despair of an endless ocean of pointless grass. We played the game many times but never found home, and that suited us just fine. Finding home wasn't the point. The point was the beautiful blood-curdling agony of it all.

When I played outside with Joe, I left the prairie behind and followed him into another classic landscape of American suffering:

The Big Woods.

We were country kids, so we knew the woods well, but these were winter woods, and winter makes many changes. It brings snow, and snow tells a story. It tattles on the animals, telling you how many there are and where they're coming from and going to. You see their tracks, craps, and burrows so easily you feel like an expert tracker. What choice do you have but to hunt for sightings of the animals themselves, all the deer, foxes, bear, and bigger game: Big Foot, Mothman, and the mutilated woodland pervs of local lore.

We sought these wonders and also the wonder of frozen ponds. Walkable ice. Pond walking made us feel like Jesus, and it made me wonder if that's what he walked on, a flat, icy path cutting through the stormy sea. Otherwise, if he was as buoyant as a cork, as the scriptures tell us, and therefore couldn't submerge himself for long, even if he dove headfirst into a wave, then what the disciples saw was a luminous man trampolining his way toward them on violent waters. They would have cried out in fear, of course, but also noted how fun it looked to be the Lord.

Joe and I found the perfect pond. It was covered in a coat of crystal-clear ice. We tested the edges. The ice held us for one second, two seconds… good enough. We rushed out onto the dark water.

When ice is clear as glass, you can see down to the weeds and the mud towns of hibernating frogs, which send up occasional, mysterious bubbles. The bubbles squish against the ice and pop, or sometimes they just sit there, staring up at you like de-skulled eyes, curious eyes, but also accusing and prophesying doom.

Farther out, the weeds and frog towns disappear, and you're locking eyes with the midnight of deep darkness.

The abyss.

There's a kind of pond in Maine that's essentially bottomless, the result of glaciers passing by long ago. Now and then a huge splinter of ice broke from a glacier and stabbed into the ground. It was driven straight down by the glacier's weight and movement, and then it broke off and was left behind. Picture mile-long daggers hammered into the Earth. In time, the daggers thawed, leaving behind ponds so deep they could swallow a sausage-link train of submarines in their sleep.

Joe and I stood in the center of the pond, staring down into that long armory of hypothermic darkness.

You know how you can only see for 7 miles on the surface of the Earth before the world curves and your sight flies off the edge in a line that goes all the way to God? Well, when it comes to pure darkness, you can only see 6 *feet* before the darkness curves and you're looking straight at Satan.

I glanced at Joe, giving my eyes a rest from Satan. "Joe?"
"What?"
"How deep do you think it is?"
We were both whispering. That's how dark the water was.
"I don't know," whispered Joe. "Could be a glacier pond."

"It *is* a glacier pond."

Our four eyes whispered the exact same sacred thing:

*bottomless*

I trembled. Joe too. And it must have been a significant vibration, because right then the ice cracked beneath our heavy boots. The crack was a single jagged line that looked like a bolt of white lightning.

"Joe!" I hissed.

"*Shut up.*"

Another crack.

Another.

If we'd thrown a long level across the surface of the pond, we would have realized the ice was sagging where we stood. For fun, imagine the fabric of spacetime sinking under the mass of two idiot moons.

A friend of mine used to be in the building-moving business. His crew hauled houses down the road on huge trailers. Sometimes, in the winter, they moved houses across frozen lakes.

But even if the ice was super thick, it still sagged under the house's weight.

The key was to keep moving. *Quickly*. Because if the house didn't move fast enough, the ice would sag so much that nothing could pull the house out of the bowl it had gotten itself into, a bowl filling with water as water filtered through the ice.

After that, there was only one thing left for the house to do:

A gleam of sunlight would flash in the upper windows, a flash of pure panic, and then the whole house would rip down through the ice and into the deeps of the lake in one big, horrifying, gurgling chug.

Joe and I were that house.

We sank on the skin of thin ice that would soon let go like a gallows' trapdoor and drop us into the bottomless grin of the Devil.

We wouldn't have died immediately, of course, but for those who found us dead, whenever they found us, it would have seemed immediate enough. For us, though, it would have felt like a long time as we froze to death trying to climb onto the ice again. Or worse: If the fall through the ice shot our bodies into the water at angles, sending us far from the hole, we would have swum up and bumped into a ceiling of ice. Against it, we'd pound our fists and die. We would become mysterious artifacts of Winter's Death Museum, our eyes staring up at the next set of children, delighting them with our prophesies of doom.

None of that happened, of course, but we didn't know that at the time. Here's what did happen: Our bodies saved us. Somehow, our bodies knew exactly what to do.

We were far too young and interesting to have stayed indoors studying the science of spreading out your weight when standing on thin substances. Therefore, the primal children lost within our modern hearts had to take over. They sent the science directly to our guts, which compelled us to hit the deck. *Gently.* To lie on our bellies on the ice. We spread ourselves out like snow angels who died awkwardly, at full splay. We spread out like bloodstains.

We waited.

The ice stopped cracking.

As we stared into the darkness beneath us, I imagined our grainy photographs in the newspaper and a well-written story about our end:

Small Town Mourns the Loss of its Meaning.

The old folks would read it and tear their garments, remembering how they should have celebrated us every time we built fires on their property, stole their lawn ornaments, and were more fascinating than their own grandchildren. Friends at school, who were only literate because they'd had no choice, wouldn't read the story, but they'd ask for a summary and then scream, "No!" and "Why them?! Why not me?!" Many children would cry bitterly, and most of them would be the girls we liked. And all children, even those who didn't know us well, would work up a sniffle and say respectfully exactly what I would have said, which would honor my memory, God bless them: "Does this mean there's no school tomorrow?"

After lying still on the ice for years, lying there attempting to be as still as stone and light as leaves, Joe and I decided to make our way from the pond's center to the edge. We slid on our bellies. We slid by the propulsion of our toes and chins, dancing the most sedate worm ever danced. It was a move I knew well, for I'd practiced with Meg endlessly, worming infinity around our little house like $19^{th}$-century children whose only toy was death.

Joe and I slithered across that prairie of ice as humbly as fallen gods, begging God for the gift that was the rest of our lives, praying he would either show us grace or mercy, whichever is the one that means you don't get what you deserve.

## LESSON 15:

# When Your Great Aunt Asks if You Want to See Her Surgery, What Choice Do You Have? You're a Kid

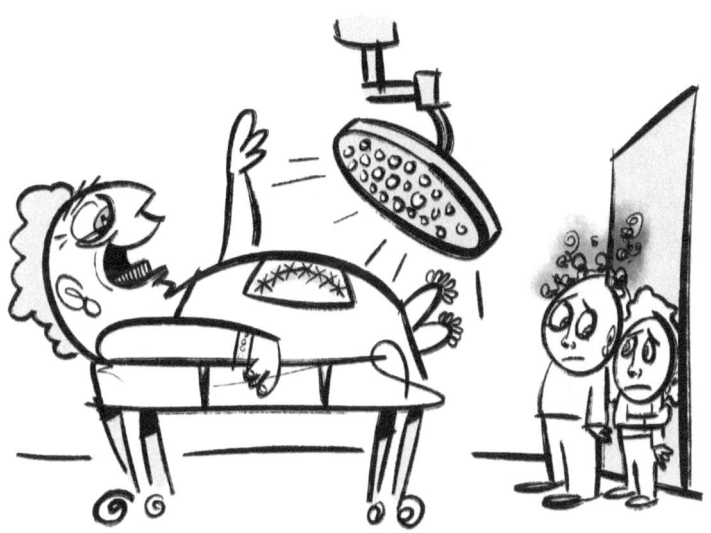

The voice came from the next room: "You kids wanna see my surgery?"

This was my Great-Aunt Corrin asking, addressing me and Meg. We would soon find out "my surgery" meant the aftermath of a surgical procedure that had taken place on the starboard side of her stomach.

By the casual and confident way she asked, she seemed to think it was an awesome question for children. But maybe all the children she'd bumped into recently were the type that demanded to see surgeries, and she was just trying to get ahead of the disrespect.

Or maybe Meg and I looked like children who were soft and in need of encounters with extremes, things that would give our characters the callouses needed for thriving in a brutal world.

Well, Aunt Corrin had just the thing.

Meg and I, standing closer together and trembling in our ancient relative's kitchen, looked at the doorway through which the voice had drifted.

We looked at each other.

Did we wanna see?

Did we really have a choice?

\*

Mom, Meg, and I had gone to Aunt Corrin's house for a visit, and for most of it, the three of us were together. But then Mom temporarily ditched us to fetch some supper. We allowed this because the supper was McDonald's.

At our house, we didn't get McDonald's. This wasn't because we were rich and could afford Wendy's. We weren't rich. It's just that Mom insisted on healthy foods.

- Not rice. Brown rice.
- Not pizza. Homemade pizza.
- Not meat. Turkey.

Hearing Mom say "McDonald's" was as surprising as cigarettes or "shit" coming out of her mouth.

Meg and I were excited.

We couldn't believe our luck. Not only were we getting McDonald's, we were getting to not eat Aunt Corrin's food, which was like real food, except it was laced with nuts, and its meat had eyes because it was olive loaf, and there was a tragic accident of celery in everything, even dessert.

Meg and I, still glowing from the McDonald's announcement, sobered up a little after the front door shut. We gave each other a look that said, *We are* here. *Here in the weird house of the oldest person we've ever known. We're here and we're...*

*alone*

We stood in that kitchen on squares of linoleum the color of abandonment, a color perfected in the 70s. We looked around at all there was to see in a house that had been lived in since the invention of despair:

- A glass-faced cabinet, the barracks of an army of salt and pepper shakers, little plastic and ceramic farm animals and children, all smiling, all with holes in their heads, execution style.

- The refrigerator's million magnets, which made it look like it died of a pustule plague.

- The ceiling light, growing a gigantic cancer of dead flies.

- Crucifixes all over the walls. Big ones. Bigger ones. Mediums. Minis. We'd never seen so much nudity.

- The sink was normal.

- But it dripped.

- It dripped the relentless rhythm of a deathwatch clock, but a clock that's slow, giving its people plenty of time to stay in the same house for a century, collecting oddments, each with a face, and positioning them so that nowhere in the house is free from the gaze of at least seventy pairs of eyes.
- Fully dilated, pitch-black eyes.
- Add paintings to the walls. So many. Paintings of condemned houses and barns, paintings of children likely dead at the time of the painting. Dead but posed in the style of the bygone world: *seen and not heard.*
- And everywhere else: framed photographs growing so fuzzy and yellow in the mud of time, photos of people who did not smile, or if they did, they looked like brain-fever cadets, smiling or laughing when there was nothing in the world to do or laugh at except winter, hunger, and dust—

And then the question from the other room:
"You kids…"
*She must mean us. We're the only kids here. No one's been kids in this house for a hundred years.*
"…wanna see…"
*Haven't we seen enough? Though maybe she's going to say, "Wanna see a cash gift?" We do.*
"…my surgery?"
Because we were children, it didn't occur to us to say, "That's very generous of you, but we'd much rather never do that ever," or say, "Aunt Corrin, we'd love to, but we don't have any surgeries of our own to show you. It just wouldn't be fair."

The only answer that occurred to us was "yes," and we gave our "yes" by walking with uncertain steps from the kitchen into the next room.

The dining room.

Where we saw Aunt Corrin lying on the dining room table.

Which can't be true.

She must have called us into the living room, not the dining room. She must have been lying on the frog-colored couch. That's where you go when you have surgeries to expose. You don't lie on dining room tables. Because that's where you dine. And that's where you will dine again, on sacred McDonald's, in fifteen to twenty minutes.

Even though she could not have been on the table, I don't have any other memory to knock this image from my head. When I asked Meg about it, she said, "I don't remember," so, believe it or not, according to what I saw, that *is* where Corrin was.

On the table.

But maybe it's not so weird. In the old times, dining room tables were often used for surgeries. They were raised surfaces, conveniently flat, and they were strong and long and wide, leaving plenty of room around the subject's body for cranial forceps, lobotomy picks, bone saws, and repurposed chamber pots: swarming with leeches. And when the amputation or hole plugging or birth was over, everyone could sit down and enjoy a hearty meal.

Aunt Corrin doing something old school on a table? Naturally. She was our Methuselah, the mascot of old school. As such, it would have been weird if she *wasn't* lying on a dining room table preparing to bare her wounds. Like the rest of us, she was a product of her times.

Meg and I entered the dining room and saw Corrin. Oh, and I forgot to mention, someone else was there with her:

A tall, gray man.

That's a lie.

I didn't forget; I withheld him until now to give you a jump scare like the one we got.

The tall, gray man was James, son of Corrin.

He was the first old man we'd ever heard of who had not moved away from his mother.

As far as I know, he grew up in that house and grew old in that house, a boy forgotten on the shelf too long, so many decades past the expiration date of youth, a tall, white-haired mystery—antiquity's child—who slept like the dead in the same room where he'd been a baby.

James wasn't a dad, an uncle, or a grandfather. He wasn't even a Mr. Corrin. He was

James and only James. That's what we were *supposed* to call him. Like he was just some kid we knew.

Saying his name, a grownup's first name, which we were taught never to do, felt disrespectful, like asking a grownup pointed, personal questions:

- "Hi, James. Why didn't you ever leave home, James?"
- "Hey, James, are you right on the edge of super creepy?"
- "What's up, James? Can your strange, stay-at-home existence be explained by a gorgeously frightening secret probably?"

Anyway, there he was, just James, hair the color of cemetery clay, height the height of a gallows for children, face the face of Corrin plus a mystery man, *the father*, Uncle Corrin, who was probably a man filling fifty canning jars under James's bed.

He stood beside the table, holding (or being held by) the hand of mother. Mother on the table. What the hell?

Also on the table: a black medical bag, a basin of water, a sponge, and rags.

Meg and I stepped into the dining room, saw what we saw, and wondered when it would happen.

When would we see the surgery?

We also had no idea what "see my surgery" meant, so we asked ourselves...

- Was James going to perform surgery while we watched?
- Was this legal?
- Would we get to see Aunt Corrin bite on a stick?
- Would James ask us if we'd like to hold one of her warm and moist (you heard me: moist) organs?
- And after we said, "Yes," because how could we say no—we were kids—would we ever recover?

But we didn't have to wait long to find out what "my surgery" meant. Without nearly enough ado, James took hold of the bottom of his mother's shirt, then he paused like an outlaw magician on the verge of revealing a crime...

- The sink dripped.
- The wind blew.
- The house's primeval bones creaked.
- One of the spiders crucified by pins on the ceiling over James's child-sized bed twitched like a tortured hand.
- A stranger not far away asked Mom, "Small, medium, or large?"
- Mom, of course, said, "Small."
- Another fly died in the kitchen light, deepening the dimness by one more death.
- James Senior's tongue shivered a little in jar number 45.
- Then James lifted his mother's shirt.

He didn't lift it all the way up to her chin—that would have made this story twice as long—but only high enough for me and Meg to see our first 89-year-old stomach.

The stomach reminded me of pizza dough, pale and limber. A liquid almost. A substance that might work best underwater, like the body of a jellyfish. Picture the graceful undulations and flappings of Aunt Corrin's stomach as it propels her from the depths of the sea up into the sunlight and onto the deck of the good ship Modern Times, alarming all the sailors.

Up went the shirt, out rolled the stomach, and there on the side of it clung an aggressively long and wide and tan bandage.

As soon as the bandage was in sight, James went for it, picking at the edge with unsurprisingly long and sharp fingernails.

He peeled it back. Yes, slowly. Yes, eyes wide on his work. Maybe swallowing and swallowing jets of arousal saliva. How should I know?

The pliant skin lifted with the bandage's stickiness. It lifted a long time, too long, before the stickiness let go—*Is he skinning her?!*

Down the length of her nose, Corrin watched the bandage and skin rise, her lips pursed in a perfect balance between love, judgement, and praise.

Then it was done. The bandage was gone.

And we saw…

A long, snarling grin of black stitches.

We saw bruising too. The bruises were multicolored. Some were colors we could have guessed: purple and blue. But there was also yellow.

There was *green*.

Not the healthy-looking green of imitation frog-skin couches.

The green of frogs proper.

Frogs proper until flattened by cars and doated to hospitals to serve in skin grafts for old ladies.

This was Aunt Corrin's surgery, and we were seeing it.

We were smelling it too.

All the smells of the hospital right there, concentrated, having been released from the hotbox of Aunt Corrin's shirt.

Imagine humid, flesh-and-chemical smells, the kind that could make Chicken McNuggets taste like the bottoms of nurses' shoes.

When James began treating the wound, cleaning it, and giving it a new bandage, he and Corrin were so focused on the job, they seemed forgetful of their audience. Meg and I took advantage of this and looked elsewhere, *anywhere* elsewhere. We hunted for an object that would save us from sucking each other's eyeballs out and swallowing them in the name of love and mercy.

There were windows to look at, but the curtains had been closed, probably for legal reasons. There was the medical bag, the sponge, the rags, but those things only reminded us of what was happening.

Then we found it.

Our eyes landed on a painting:

*The Last Supper.*

It shouldn't have taken us that long to find it. The painting was huge. You could easily (Thank God) get lost in it, so we did. While the wound care went on and on, we stared long and hard at that old supper.

We studied Jesus and the boys, the fellowship and feasting, the beautiful colors—blue, purple, yellow, green.

We prayed:

*Dear God, why did you guys use only one side of that table? If you'd used both sides, you could have gotten a much smaller table and saved money. Being on one side only is probably why everybody was doing all that famous leaning. They couldn't hear each other. Is that what pissed off Judas? I hate repeating myself too. Or maybe he did what he did because he thought you wanted him to. You said, "Hey, Judas, how about DON'T do it? Don't do what you're thinking of doing," but after it telephoned its way down to him from apostle to apostle, what he heard was "Judas... do it." But we're grateful for how you organized the supper anyway. Otherwise, there'd be no painting, and we'd have sucked our eyes out by now, for thine is the kingdom and the power and the glory forever and ever, amen.*

And even though we knew betrayal was in the air, that old supper was exactly where we wanted to be: thousands and thousands of miles away, at a table covered with bread, wine, and fruit cups, and not a surgery in sight.

How lovely it would be to sit at that table, we thought: reclining, leaning, feasting with some of the most famous people in the world, and ratting on Judas, repeating ourselves, "*I said, GET JUDAS!*" and getting to crucify *him* for once.

As I stared at the painting, it occurred to me that I had a bigger question for Jesus than my seating-arrangement question. In fact, I had a monster of a question, and I was about to ask him when Aunt Corrin called out, "There we go!"

We looked at her again.

Her shirt was down.

The show was over.

"Good as new," she said, and James grinned like a recently unearthed skull.

And because we'd been raised right, we said, "Thank you."

\*

At long last, Mom returned with food and asked me and Meg, "Were you well behaved?"

"Yes," we said, then quietly, "even though no one else was."

"What was that?" said Mom.

"Nothing."

During supper, while we all sat around *the* dining room table, while I plucked nugget after nugget from the bloodbath of ketchup in my nugget box, I tried my best to think of nothing. I sent myself far away by staring once again at the painting.

Its blues and purples.

Yellows.

*The* greens!

*Don't think! I beg you, think of **nothing**, please. Don't you dare compare nugget meat to anything but nugget meat! Think instead of family, of the kindness of great-aunts who open their homes to visitors, share their tables, are humble enough to allow nieces to treat them to suppers, and are kind enough to bare the* *brutal truth of life to the rising generations while there's still time. Think of mothers who make sure the doors of home stay open forever for their children. Think of good sons who care for their mothers through thick, thin, and stitches. Think of people as people, as so much more than ghoulish vessels for catching the nightmarish contents of the festering wound you call a mind.*

But I was way too young to think of so many things.

I looked and looked at the painting.

By the artist's design, my eyes locked on Jesus, and I remembered my question for him.

The big one.

Even bigger than before.

Because it was now a question for myself and Meg as well. For James too, and Aunt Corrin.

As I ate my nuggets and stared at the Lord, knowing what had happened to him after that supper, knowing what had happened to Aunt Corrin moments before *our* supper, I finally asked my question:

*How the hell can you* eat at a time like this?

# LESSON 16:

# If You Have a Song to Sing, Sing It. Damn the Danger

A pirate is this: "A sea-thief, one who without authority and by violence interferes with the property of another upon the sea…"

*

Once upon a time on a Saturday morning, I was kayaking in Branch Pond, a big pond in Maine. I discovered if I parked my kayak in the water 200 yards from the old grist mill and sang like a whale, my song echoed majestically off the mill.

So, I parked my kayak 200 yards out and sang. I loved my voice as it bounced off the mill gigantically and traveled out over the pond, the water adding power to the sound. The grist mill was as good as a funhouse mirror: It turned a small boy into a giant, a giant so in love with his larger-than-life voice that he sang whale song for over an hour.

Suddenly, I heard from the far end of Branch Pond, the sound of an engine. It hacked and gargled to life then began a monotone roar, such an ugly, unnatural sound. Sound pollution. I wondered why people couldn't just let me have a quiet day on the pond. If I'd known Jean-Paul Sartre back then, I would have agreed with him:

"Hell *is* other people."

The engine got louder, and soon I saw a little boat. It was heading my way.

*Fast.*

I thought, *There's no boat landing around here. I wonder what they're up to. Maybe they're just people who* really *like getting to their fishing spot. At forty miles an hour.*

As the boat boated closer, I saw its people: a driver and a boy.

The driver was a man bound only by a tank top, camouflage pants, and a combative haircut (flat on top, bald on the sides and back), the haircut of soldiers and worse: wannabe soldiers. The boy had propped himself up in the bow like the figurehead of an old-timey ship, except he didn't look like a topless mermaid. He was fully topped and looked furious. They both did.

*If fishing makes you that angry*, I thought, why even do it?

The boat was a hundred feet away, fifty feet, fifteen, and heading right for me. I thought briefly I might have to leap from my kayak to avoid getting run over. But before this could happen, the boat veered to my left side, came around, and started circling me. *Close.* Making waves and bigger waves, threatening to swamp my kayak.

While the boat circled, the father and son yelled at me. I couldn't hear the words over the engine, but their mouths had an f-word look. This was a look and word I knew well. But I never thought to say it back to them. To me, the f-word was a word you said when you were completely alone in the bathroom. You whispered it at the mirror. This didn't stop God from hearing and seeing it, but I'd learned when it came to whispering in the bathroom, he let you get away with murder.

Since a conversation with the man and boy was impossible because of engine noise and my puritanical f-word rules, which wouldn't allow me to establish any verbal common ground, there was nothing for me to do but fight against the swamping waves and win. In fact, I played in the waves. I played like an otter, an otter in a kayak, an otter capable of whale song and self-absorption to the point of having no idea how he's affecting the serene Saturday morning world around him. It was fun. I raced up the waves and howled with happiness as I coasted down the other side.

The father and son, failing to do anything but add to my good time, eventually boated away. However, as they left, the child extended both arms, and with his longest fingers, he sent a message. The message contained a few questions and answers. With his fingers, he was asking, "Why did my father and I take the time to load up the boat and come to the pond today? For fishing. Any other reason? Yes. For the fun of being outdoors after a long week of school for me and a longer week of work for him. And why didn't we bring a radio with us or fireworks? Because there's just something special about the quiet of the natural world, a quiet full of the gentle sound of waves against a drifting boat, the sound of breezes in tall pines, the lonesome call of a faraway hawk, the splash of a jumping fish, a promise of success. This kind of quiet is more than special; it's the kind that fills a person up until they can't remember what it was that made them feel so discouraged about their lives just yesterday, the kind of quiet that makes me and my father almost friends, for once. That's it, I guess. The reason we're out here. It's the quiet and how the quiet heals our breaking hearts." That was one of his fingers. The other one said, "What we *don't* come to the pond for is to hear a sick kid screaming like insane animals for an hour. In other words, Fuck you! Fuck you very much!"

His fingers were really good at communicating, so I understood him quickly, and I did feel bad. A little. Bad enough that I didn't sing like a whale for the rest of that afternoon. I didn't even sing like a boy. I became so quiet that those two guys should have come back to thank me for making myself a part of the sacred quiet that healed them. They never did, though, which makes sense. They seemed like the type of people who excel at telling someone what they're doing wrong, but never get around to telling them what they're doing so right.

I paddled in the quiet, listening to waves, wind, birds, flopping fish, and so forth. It was the kind of quiet that allows a boy to grow his hatreds. I hated the father and son. I hated them, *and* I felt bad for what I'd done, both at the same time. I contain multitudes, which includes whales, as you know.

Years later, when I happened to come across the definition of "pirate," I remembered that day on the pond, long ago. Because on that day, wasn't I "one who without authority and by violence interferes with the property of another upon the sea"?

What was the property of the boating blood-buddies, the offensive daddy and his long-fingered seed?

Peace and quiet.

What was I? A watery thief. One who without authority used the violence of 900 consecutive catcalls of whales to interfere.

So, what is a pirate?

A pirate, my friends, is me.

your doodles, memories, illustrations, story ideas...

**LESSON 17:**

# Older Brothers Giveth, But Not Without First Takething a Lot Away

When my parents bought a Nintendo Entertainment System (NES) in the late '80s, Joe, Meg, and I became idolaters, worshipers of the machine.

Especially Joe.

One Saturday morning, early, Meg and I ran an experiment on him, one that would tell us just how deeply he'd swallowed the hooks of our new household god.

Joe was still asleep, lost behind his locked door, dead asleep in the black-out-curtain darkness of his chamber. With Meg at my side, I turned on the game and muted the volume. We could see his door from the TV room and kept an eye on it while giggling into our hands and turning up the volume from zero to one, then one to two, and so on.

At level five, which is hardly noticeable by dogs, Joe opened his door. With his eyes still closed, his mouth grinning sleepily, and his body mummified in blankets, he dream-walked to the TV room. Yes, he used the game's music to echolocate himself to his place of worship without injury. He looked asleep because he was asleep. He didn't wake up until he had the controller in hand and was halfway through level two. I have a feeling if he'd coded out in his bedroom that morning, we could have skipped the shock paddles, cranked Mario, and Joe would have played his way back to life.

We got the NES at a time when Meg was so young that she played as if the point of the game was to kill Mario. In my slightly-older hands, Mario was only a little bit safer. But under Joe's command, Mario was a monster, a pixelated Angel of Death who turned the Mushroom Kingdom into a mass grave of Goombas, Koopa Troopas, Piranha Plants, and Bullet Bills. Without question, Joe had the talent to fight his way through all eight worlds of the kingdom then burst into King Koopa's castle and stomp him to death in his bedroom.

He could do it, but only if he was allowed to play long enough, only if he didn't have to stop after fifteen minutes, the length of one play session according to the freshly minted game-laws of our parents. Other game laws:

- No rage-twisting the controller until it creaks and cracks.

- No beating the chair with the controller.

- No using the controller as a knife and stabbing the TV.
- No swearing.
- No punching or kicking.
- No spitting.
- No screaming or crying.
- No jumping up and down and clapping when your siblings can't stop dying.

Though the law of fifteen minutes guaranteed sharing, it was a particularly nasty arrangement in those old and brutal days, back when saving your progress in your own personal game was impossible. You had to beat the entire game in one fell swoop or not at all, and not even Joe could do that in 15 minutes.

He needed more time.

He needed *our* time.

And though Meg and I valued our turns deeply and dearly, we also wanted to watch Koopa's execution more than we wanted to see heaven, which was saying a lot considering the hours we'd spent designing heaven: a place with pizza forests, Mountain Dew rivers, and Mattel View-Masters mounted on every golden street corner so we could frequently check in on our teachers in hell.

The conundrum: keep our turns and never see the end of the game, or give our turns to the master and witness Koopa's defeat?

In the presence of Joe's ability, our wills weakened. We watched him slaughter and unearth secrets. We told him, "You're *so* good."

He smiled. "This I know."

"You could beat the game!"

"I believe you." Silence. He allowed our minds to do what he knew our minds were doing.

We watched him murder 16 Goombas in a row. He hopped from skull to skull without touching the ground. We gasped. We wiggled with overstimulation. Joe sighed. "I'd *love* to beat the game, but there's just not enough time. Darn it!" He punched his leg dramatically and gently. "If only there was a way…"

In our heads, we said no, we said never. Who would ever give up their turn? But then our galloping hearts overrode our heads and spoke: "Okay."

"Okay, what?" he asked.

"You can…" I stopped. Meg put her hand on my shoulder to strengthen me. I shuddered. "You can… have our turns."

"Is this really what you want?" he asked.

Meg and I looked at each other. Of course it wasn't what we wanted. And of course it was. We were trapped by our desire, our need. We nodded.

"Yes," I said, "but you have to beat the game *right now*. Can you?"

"Perhaps," he said.

"Please!" we wailed.

"I don't know." He yawned. "I'm pretty tired."

He wasn't tired. With a Nintendo controller in his hand, he could lie on a bed of Maleficent spindles and not even feel drowsy.

"For the love of God," we begged, "we're begging you! We'll do absolutely anything, even the unthinkable. For example, we're giving you our turns! Can you beat the game today or not?! *Will* you beat it?!"

Joe paused his game to think. He looked around the room. He tapped his finger on his lips, deep in thought. Then he seemed to notice he was sitting on the floor. "I'm going to need a chair, I think. Yes, Mom's rocking chair."

We ran to get it. We ran back with it, decimating door frames, decimating our shins by accidental chair kicks. We placed it in front of the TV.

Joe repositioned the chair, repositioned it again, sat, then went back to thinking. "Now... I believe I'd like a drink. In a tall glass."

We ran for the kitchen, but he snapped his fingers. "Stop!" We stopped. "Come back." We came back. "Have I told you what I'd *like* to drink yet?"

We stood before him. Waiting.

He waited.

Finally, we figured out what he was waiting for and asked him, "What would you like to drink?"

"Good question." He pondered again.

How long would we have to wait to see Koopa die? How long *could* we wait? Don't be ridiculous, we could wait a century. Still, we suffered.

Eventually, Joe spoke unto us, saying, "I would like milk. I would like milk in a glass. A tall glass. *Cold* milk."

We flew and fetched his milk then returned to find Joe rocking in the rocking chair, smacking his lips. He reached for the milk. We gave. "Prepare the game," he said.

We looked at him, we looked at the TV. The game was already prepared. "What do you mean?"

He groaned. His patience was all but gone. "Turn it off, take the game out, put it away, then set it all up again. If I'm going to do this, I want to do it from the very, *very* beginning. Or it won't count."

Though we didn't understand, we did as he asked, turning off the NES, removing the game cartridge, returning it to its protective sleeve, then taking it out again, and putting it back into the NES. But before we could put it back in, Joe said, "Stop! You have to blow on it."

He was right. We'd forgotten. Part of the NES activation ceremony was blowing on the open end of the game cartridge before inserting it into the machine. Though no one knew why, everyone knew of the importance of this step. It had to be done. And there was precedent. We'd seen people on TV blow on dice before rolling and blow on guns after shooting. It was just how the world worked back then.

Meg and I aimed the cartridge's open end toward our faces and filled our lungs, but before we could blow, Joe hollered, "Wait! You'll just spit in it. Bring it to me."

We obeyed. We held the cartridge in the air, waiting for him to take it. He didn't.

"Bring it to my *lips*."

Again, we obeyed, and when the cartridge was an inch from his lips, he sent into it a dry wind.

"Now," he said, "load it."

Finally, it was happening. We loaded the cartridge, our fingers trembling. We handed Joe the controller. He accepted. We pressed the "power" button, and the game began. All was ready. All he had to do now was select "1 Player Game" and go!

But when he didn't, we looked at him and saw that all *wasn't* ready. He smacked his lips again.

"Cookies," he said. "Cookies would be nice. I'll need the energy."

We hesitated. A pulse of rebellion beat in our guts suddenly. Or it did in mine. Meg stopped hesitating and was gone, running for the pantry. She came back with cookies.

Now Joe had the chair, the milk, the blown cartridge, the inserted cartridge, the controller, the power pressed, the cookies…

*Now*, at long last, it would begin.

But it didn't yet.

Joe considered. Again, he looked all around. What was missing? He closed his eyes to think. Then his eyes popped open.

*He knew.*

"Are you guys cold?" he said. We didn't know where he'd learned to give indirect commands, but we knew enough about the practice to understand what he meant. He meant the room was cold and we should do something about it. So, we delivered a blanket and covered his legs.

Then, after so much work and waiting, so much sacrifice and longing, we got what we wanted:

Joe began.

And for the next two hours and fifty minutes, Meg and I sat on either side of our talented brother, handing him milk, handing him cookies, adjusting his blanket, rocking his chair for him or holding it still, and watching him curb stomp the life out of every Koopa goon in sight, then storm the last castle, send the hammer-juggling king himself to the pit where the worm dieth not, and rescue at long last the great lady of our waiting, the culmination of all our hope and longing:

Princess Toadstool herself.

When it was over, Meg and I lost our minds with excitement, jumping up and down, clapping, hollering, and singing spontaneous psalms of conquest.

Joe, on the other hand, was silent.

He rose slowly from the rocking chair, draped the blanket over his shoulders like the cape of a warrior emperor, then strode away, leaving us to clean up his cookie crumbs and dishes, and to return Mom's heavy chair, reopening our shin wounds; leaving us to spend the rest of the day outside in the cold because we'd spent every last second of our precious game time on someone else's victory.

And we thanked him for it.

And thanked him again.

your doodles, memories, illustrations, story ideas...

# LESSON 18:

# There's No Such Thing as an Unconditional Crush

I'm in the air. I'm upside down. I'm falling from my grandparents' maple tree.

A moment before this, I'd been hanging from a branch by the backsides of my knees. Then, somehow, I slipped. Next, I fell in accordance with the rules of cruel nature: straight down, headfirst.

Just before I struck the ground with the top of my head, my right arm made itself a hero, diving in the way, getting between my skull and the Earth. It provided a soft landing-place for my head, which took advantage of this. Too much advantage. My head hit my arm as hard as a war hammer would do it and snapped the bone four inches above the wrist.

I vaguely remember my upside-down flight, but I clearly remember my stumble-run back to Grammy and Grampa's house. According to my vision at that time, a vision framed by a soupy ring of darkness, I ran along the surface of a world tipping left and right, a world hoping to slide me off the edge of the map. The unsteady, out-of-joint planet made my run wiggly and serpentine while my eyes added to the mix a veil of tear-blindness. Still, I was close enough to the house that I couldn't get lost, not even blind, not even tossed by a lawn that wasn't a lawn; it was a stormy sea, and I was a boy carved out of cork. By angels, muscle memory, and the momentum of pain, I found the front door at last.

The family put me on a couch in my favorite room. We the children had a name for the room: "the death room" or "the room of death." It was where the previous owner had died. That's all we knew about the previous owner; he died in that room, on that couch. This wasn't true, of course, the couch part. You don't keep a couch of the dead, especially if you didn't know the guy—also, couches are sponges, and the dead leak—but we the children would have none of this; either the old man died on that very couch, or nothing else in our world was true. Because we loved and needed the mystique the dead old man added to the room *and* the couch. What a gift. We played there as often as we could, feeling young, which means immortal, telling ghost stories, and taking turns being the dead old man. It was easy; you just had to lie there under a blanket then jump up and chase whoever dared to get close enough to touch the bump of your dead nose.

However, death rooms aren't as fun when you're injured. You begin wondering if this room is suddenly the worst one in the house. It has bad luck. Maybe the previous owner was injured too. Maybe his family put him here to rest, and that's what killed him: the room. The couch. Because evil can live in things as easily as it can live in people. Demons in the Bible hitched rides in pigs and idols. Maybe the demons of our time live at grandparents' houses, in the walls, floors, and ceilings of certain rooms. They live in couches. But this doesn't change their appetites:

They want souls.

So, while I lay there in pain, the room and couch whispering assurances of death, the family crowded around, trying to figure out what was wrong with my arm. I couldn't stop cradling it and hissing when Mom and Dad attempted to pull up my sweatshirt sleeve to see the damage.

If it had been the old days, the family would have given me a stick to bite while they yanked up my sleeve and set the broken bones. Next, they'd have given me a splint to wear, a splint made of other sticks. After that, if I still hissed and howled, they would have whipped me with all the rest of the sticks lying around. And though we did have sticks aplenty, it wasn't the old days, thank God. It was modern times, the enlightened times in which medicinal sticks are used to build hospitals, so that's where we went.

At the hospital, because we couldn't figure out how to pull up my sweatshirt sleeve without me screaming, a nurse cut the sleeve off with little shining scissors. The sweatshirt was an early 90s design: zany shapes of all colors chased by long squiggles and coils, a microscopic snapshot of some terminal disease dance party. My greatest shirt. Ruined. I was at my best—funniest, most adventurous while wearing it. I would just have to find a way to have a personality without it.

Once the sleeve was gone, we got a shock.

The arm traveled along normally enough from the elbow to about halfway down, but then it went wrong and *very* wrong. The bones had broken so badly, my arm seemed to have developed a second elbow. Gasps filled the room. And though my arm hurt in a way I'd never felt before—oddly, the pain was as sharp as a handful of cat teeth and broken glass, but also as numb as death—I did feel a little rush; I'd done something all by myself that was so extreme it had the same effect on family *and* strangers: It took their breath away.

Life's mission: accomplished.

Once I was done captivating all the people, medical folks put me in a wheelchair and rolled me away. I ended up on a bed in a room under searing lights. Mom and Dad were nowhere to be seen. Orphan Danny. A pretty lady forced a fighter pilot's mask onto my face. I fought her, but I couldn't fight the mask gasses. Lady Lovely said, "Count to ten." I made it to three, which isn't bad considering how difficult it is to count while fighting, inhaling chemicals, and falling in love.

If I dreamed, I dreamed of telling all my friends about the nurse, my very own Mrs. Robinson: "Boys, she likes a man in a mask. It seems her dead husband was a fighter pilot." And I dreamed of my other girlfriend, Maggy Marston. Oh, the pain she'd feel when I introduced my nurse. Poor Mags. I had leveled up. My little M&M would now have to compete with grown women.

In dreams and out of them, I couldn't wait to bring my broken arm to school. At Palermo Consolidated School, wounded kids were celebrities. A broken leg, skinless knuckles, missing teeth: all evidence that you had lived and lived well. Which I had. More than that, I'd flown. I'd climbed for the summit of Babel, fallen into my own cautionary tale, and best of all, I'd lived to tell it.

The cast, my friends, was blue and bold: It went from my elbow all the way to my hand. I was Exoskeleton Boy. My power? Break me, and my girlfriend who is a woman wraps me in moldable, hardening fiberglass, making me even stronger, making me more and more a *man*.

At school, my wishes came true. The children paid me tribute, organizing themselves into a cast-signing line that snaked across the classroom.

They signed with markers, with crayons, with aromatic Sharpies. My mind expanded on the fumes. I saw the signing line stretching out into miles, and I heard voices:

"I wish *I* could break a bone."

"Forget it. No one breaks bones like *him*."

Word would spread, leading to television interviews. Offers. "Should we make a movie of his life?"

"What do you mean, 'should we'?"

"You're right. Forgive me. We'll start immediately."

I'd become a face on t-shirts and cereal boxes, a mural on the sides of buildings in depressed cities, bringing hope to all: "You can drop us from the sky, break our arms, but you can't stop us. *We are Dan*." I'd become action figures, plushies, muscular rubber dolls, and every toy of me would have bones you could break then wrap in blue armor. Imagine all the money, if you can. Now double it.

But there was a downside: Casts make you itch.

I scratched my hidden arm with knitting needles, fishing rods, marshmallow spears, and a craving fork. The relief was heavenly, technically my sexual awakening. To this day, I go hot-cold just looking at the suggestively long and nimble handles of flyswatters.

I itched because I was healing, and I itched because my healing arm and the cast were increasingly filthy. Before long, the arm became my Dorian Gray portrait, expressing all the foulness of the inner boy, a boy who would have broken his whole head off to be an action figure, an idol, a star.

It wasn't long before the cast-signing days were history. Kid after kid backed away from my fumes. And finally, so did my Maggy Marston. I noticed she stopped standing downwind of me, and eating around me, and being around me. I don't blame her. She had a lot on her mind. She had a big decision to make. On the one hand, I had a few nice qualities: good looks, athleticism, hilarity, brilliance, power. On the other, I had that *smell.*

She delivered her decision during recess, handing me a note then running away, upwind.

It went like this:

*Dear Dan,*
 *Are we broken up now?*

Beneath the question, she'd drawn a little box with the word "**YES**" hovering over it. There was a "**NO**" box too. And though her question had been addressed to me, she'd gone ahead and answered it, checking the **YES** box with a check so deep and dark her little wooden desk still bears the checkmark scar.

I looked up from the note and saw her standing on the other side of the playground, so far away from me she was in another school district.

To my shame, I asked her why it was over. This was before I learned one of the great truths of romance: Never ask why. Instead, while someone's dumping you, celebrate, no matter how much it hurts. This shows your strength and fills ex-lovers with regret.

Go, and do likewise.

But like I said, I hadn't yet learned these survival skills. So, I asked why. Though my ex and I were geographically far from one another, I did my best to get some answers:

**DAN**: Why?
**MAGGY**: What?
**DAN**: Why?!

**MAGGY**: I can't hear you!

**DAN**: What?!

**MAGGY**: I can't *hear* you!

**DAN**: Oh. Sorry.

**MAGGY**: What?!

**DAN**: I said *WHY*?!

**MAGGY**: It's your arm!

**DAN**: What?!

**MAGGY**: Your *arm!*

**DAN**: My *what*?!

**MAGGY**: ARM! ARM! YOUR ARM!

**DAN**: What about it?

**MAGGY**: What?

**DAN**: I SAID, what ABOUT my arm?

**MAGGY**: IT'S YOUR *ARM!* IT REALLY, *REALLY* STINKS!

**DAN**: Oh.

**MAGGY**: What?

**DAN**: I said, OH!

**MAGGY**: I CHECKED "YES" FOR YOU! THAT MEANS WE'RE BROKEN UP!

**DAN**: FINE!

**MAGGY**: BECAUSE OF YOUR ARM —

**DAN**: *OKAY!*

**MAGGY**: IT JUST SMELLS SO INCREDIBLY BAD, YOU KNOW?! LIKE I WANT TO THROW UP! I'VE SMELLED TONS OF BAD THINGS IN MY LIFE, BELIEVE ME, BUT NOTHING LIKE YOUR ARM! THAT'S

WHY WE'RE BROKEN UP! DID YOU SEE THAT I CHECKED YES?!

**DAN**: Yes.

**MAGGY**: WHAT?!

**DAN**: Yes!

**MAGGY**: I CAN'T HEAR YOU!

**DAN**: YES! YES! I SEE, *I SEE!*

So, I decided to give her some space and to dream of my nurse picking me up from school in front of everyone, her full-on woman beauty making them all suffer.

For the rest of recess, I played a game of tag, running from my arm's colony of flies. As I ran, I realized there's no such thing as unconditional romantic loyalty. You must perform. No messing up. Be perfect or it's over. And heaven forbid some innocent part of you takes on a subtle, slightly challenging aroma, one that a true love could get used to if they possessed the proper depth of character.

I looked at my cast and its many names ("Maggie Marston" included), names intended by their signers to secure for them a share of my glory. But now the names turned my cast into a petition, one requesting my banishment, a banishment that would be in force so long as I continued smelling like a rotting boy.

Eventually, the cast came off. I welcomed back into the world a thin, pale arm, which I immediately began to repair, covering it with sunburns, muscles, and knife wounds. Before long, Maggy returned. They all did.

But I kept the cast.

I buried it in a shoebox in the darkness of my closet. Like a bad memory, it continued stinking long after the event that created it.

Not only did it keep its stink, it kept those names, the names of all my friends and the love of my life.

Over and over as the years went by, I'd lock my door, dig out the cast, give it a sniff, and try it on. I'd squeeze my arm into the thing until it hurt, until it seemed impossible that the cast and its stench could ever have belonged to me.

The worse it fit, the better I felt. The more it hurt—the more the cast seemed to say, *You are not the boy I know. Where is he? Where is Rot Boy?*—the braver I became, brave enough to toss the bad memory back into the dark, to leave my room and be the boy I knew, the one I'd always been no matter what the past had to say about it, a boy no one would ever banish, a boy back in trees, back in the sky, flying, and why not?

After all, he is young, he smells of the strongest soaps, and he is loved unconditionally.

## LESSON 19:

# Attempted Murder Doesn't Make You a Failure. At Least You Tried, Which is More Than Most People Can Say

My brother and I were in the driveway arguing about dinosaurs.

**ME**: I like dinosaurs.

**JOE**: I like them more—

**ME**: I *hate* you!

See how easy it was for Joe to rile me up in those days? I was a bull. He was a bull scientist.

**SCIENTIST**: How about this one? (holds up a green cape)

**BULL**: I don't like it.

**SCIENTIST**: And this one? (yellow cape)

**BULL**: You know I have an anger problem, right?

**SCIENTIST**: How about (continues flipping through the laboratory cape rack) *this* one?

(This cape is, of course, red.)

**BULL**: (Chases scientist with horns. It's attempted murder. However, BULL is later acquitted due to temporary insanity.)

I often got in trouble for my outbursts. For example: Joe would run crying to Mom and show her a dent in his body about the size and shape of a violently thrown toy, a ten-pound metal dump truck. I would explain that I'd thrown the truck because I had to.

"*Why* did you have to?" Mom would say.

- Because Joe drew a better ninja than me.
- Joe skipped a rock better than me.
- Joe saved his Halloween candy way longer than I ever could. I loved my body way too much to withhold candy from it for even an instant—

"These aren't reasons," Mom would say. "You get upset too easy." Then I'd be punished.

But eventually Mom investigated my violent reactions to find out why I kept going wild for such small reasons. She listened in on our play, and that's when she heard an endless stream of a certain kind of talk from Joe:

- You think you can do things?
- You can't do things.
- You're stupid.

- You can't do *anything*.
- Let's see your drawing.
- You call that a ninja?
- I call it "crap." It sucks.
- Let's skip rocks now.
- Check *this* skip out.
- Your turn.
- Wow, you suck at rock skipping too?
- Oh well, let's take a candy break. Oops, your candy's gone, isn't it. Probably because you're worthless? Just an educated guess. Hey, but you can lick my wrappers like human garbage if you want to.

    Mom learned my violence wasn't because Joe could draw better than me, skip rocks better, and still have Halloween candy in January like a masochist. These things were just last straws, devastating to me only because of what preceded them: Joe's powerful words. Words crafted with care. He was a wordsmith who worked like a key maker, filing his language into little blades with teeth on them, marvelous for unlocking the safe where I kept my mortal fears and agonies.

    For some reason, I didn't think to tell on him constantly for his discouraging words. Instead, my rage would build, and then he'd tie his shoes faster than me or mispronounce my name, saying "Dan" with a special accent that made it sound like "Moron," and I'd attack. Afterwards, I'd claim and actually believe it was the shoe tying that made me do it; it was the "Moron;" but Mom, after her investigations, knew better.

    As a result, Joe's punishments increased in number, and my life became almost a joy. The days, months, and years murmured along somewhat balanced, relatively stable, and I planned to go to the grave like that, living in a world of equal punishment, a world of fairness.

But then the day arrived that Joe forged an insult which would become the king of insults for me, a single bit of verbal fire that could bring about a meltdown all by itself. No build up. No last straw.

Just one fell and devastatingly effective swoop.

The insult was "Fat Boy." As in, "You suck at stuff, Fat Boy." I would hear it and explode on cue like Old Faithful. You could set your watch on my Fat Boy furies.

**And now, I offer the dreaded history of "Fat Boy."**

Once upon a Friday night, Palermo Consolidated School was having a sleepover in the school itself, a sleepover for us, the children of the fourth grade. I was terribly excited. That entire week, for thousands and thousands of minutes, I did nothing but imagine the freedom on the way: every nine and ten-year-old of my world running up and down the halls all night, screaming, battling, playing endless games of Bloody Mary and Summon the Devil, consuming buckets of soda and candy, drawing filth on the chalkboards, hunting the ghosts of dead children and dead teachers, and our only chaperone was our teacher, a hippy lady who made us feel especially free because she didn't believe in God or consequences.

Halfway through the event, deep in the night, someone decided all the boys should take off their shirts and parade around. With fourth graders, ideas turn to actions so fast the ideas and actions occur at the same instant. A fourth-grade idea is a doctor's reflex hammer hitting a knee. The knee is the fourth grader's body, his everything. The hammer hits, the knee kicks. It will, it must, if the fourth grader is alive. So, when his mind thinks of something to say, his mouth is saying it, and when his mind thinks of something to do, it's done.

After the shirtless idea struck, the boys thought about it, which is to say, we were shirtless. We moved in a pack for safety, standing very close together, a churning pack, which sent those standing on the inside to the outer edges for their turn to be observed by the girls. The rotation continued. We were an organism born to turn itself inside out every thirty seconds or so.

No one escaped their turn in the spotlight.

Sadly, the wonderfully free sleepover came to an end, but it had been everything I'd hoped for. I thought of the hallway races and screaming, the battles and horror games, the sugar madness, the ghosts, our good and godless teacher, and I smiled all Saturday and Sunday.

However, it turns out Rhonda Davis, the most popular girl in fourth grade, had submitted a message about me to the grapevine, which was a vast spiderweb in our town, a message that had been shivering its way toward me along the sticky silken threads all weekend. I received it Monday morning.

The messenger: a short, cold-sore bearing boy named Ben. He found me at recess.

I said, "Hi." I said it happily, not knowing my life was about to change forever.

Instead of saying "Hi" back, he said, "Rhonda Davis said something about you."

I told you Rhonda was popular, but she was more than that. She was a commander, a child who could save you with a smile then break you with an eyeroll, a kid so powerful she'd told Trent Valentine to carve her name into his wrist with a thumbtack then fill the wound with pen ink to make a tattoo, and Trent had done it.

I wondered what Rhonda had said. Maybe it was something good. Maybe she'd said, "Inform Dan that I'd like him to be even more popular from now on. He doesn't have to do anything. I'll do it. In fact, *it is done*. All he has to do is prepare to be celebrated." I would have accepted immediately. I would have had no choice.

A little thrilled, a little nervous, I asked Ben to deliver Rhonda's message.

He did: "She said you're fat."

Now and then, there's a moment in swordfight movies when one fighter cuts the other one in half, but it's such a clean cut, and so fast, the dead one doesn't immediately realize he's dead. He blinks with confusion, knowing at the very least that *something* just happened, though he's not sure what, not until the enemy gives him a nudge and he falls to the ground in two pieces.

That's what it was like. I walked away, blinking rapidly, looking exactly like a boy who was all one piece, but I wasn't, not anymore. In fact, the slightest push, if it had to do with me and fat, would make me fall to pieces.

Rhonda's message hit me so hard because it was just as surprising as it was hurtful. So surprising that I had no defenses against it. It flew unchallenged right to the dead center of me. If she'd called me stupid, annoying, boring, worthless, a moron, or human garbage, I would have blocked her better. I knew those attacks well. But it had never occurred to me that I, a member of an exceptionally thin and athletic family, was fat, or even *could* be fat. Unfortunately, since receiving Rhonda's message, it's never stopped occurring to me. The thread she strummed is still shivering, still delivering, even though fourth grade is long gone. I imagine her as an enemy soldier, a radio operator who was lost, left behind, and forgotten on some faraway island. The war is over. It ended forever ago, but not for her. She doesn't know. Her radio is broken, so she can only transmit, not receive. And she does transmit, because even though she's the enemy, she's a good soldier. She sends out her demoralizing propaganda every day and will never stop. And though *I* know the war is over, I still won't take my shirt off in public for any reason. Not for a waterpark. Not for a bird dropping. Not even if the shirt was on fire. And you can't make me.

After that day, Joe noticed something about me was different, and he needed to figure out what it was. What made me say, "No, thank you" to second helpings at supper? What made me start jogging? And why was I lifting weights at the age of 10? He sent exploratory depth charges into my deeps to find the answer:

Watching me run, he said, "You can't run. You're slow. Slow boy!"

I told him to shut up. I told him to die. But I didn't seem upset enough to him. And I didn't stop running.

He watched me lift weights. "You're not strong at all," he said. "You're weak. Weak boy!"

I ignored him. I kept lifting.

He watched me *very* carefully at mealtimes. "You don't eat as much anymore. Is it because you suck at eating?"

"Shut up! I'm the *best* at eating!"

And then his eyes widened and brightened. "Wait," he said, "I know! Oh my gosh, I know
what it is! You think you're fat! You're FAT BOY!"

That got the reaction he was looking for. I lost my mind.

"Fat Boy" was a magic term. It was light, well-balanced, and easy to throw with perfect accuracy. It was Joe's masterpiece. 100% effective in large doses (shouted) or small doses (whispered). All he had to do was say it, "Hey, Fat Boy," and every single time, I'd pause my run, set down my weights, push my dinner plate away, and erupt.

Joe didn't use his perfect weapon often because it got him in big trouble—Mom and Dad were increasingly worried about me working out too much, eating too little, and spending so long in front of mirrors, spinning around slowly like a demon-possessed head—but he did use it. And it's hard to blame him. He was the inventor and owner of a button that made extremely interesting and satisfying things happen to his enemy, and he was a kid. What kid wouldn't push a button like that? It was almost cruel of Mom and Dad to tell him not to. Repressing such a powerful and natural urge can warp a kid forever.

Joe and I were on the front lawn, going back and forth between hitting pinecones with wiffle bats and popping wheelies with our bikes. He popped one. I attempted one and failed. He laughed then tried to tell me how to succeed. I said, "Shut up." I said it even though we weren't allowed to.

Joe glared at me. "Don't tell me to shut up."

"Shut up," I said.

"*Don't* say it."

"Shut up" was the closest thing I had to a "Fat Boy" of my own, a weapon that could actually bother him.

"Shut up," I said again.

"I'm warning you."

"I don't care. Shut *up*."

He smiled a little, his eyes bright with the fun of giving in to a big temptation. Then he said it: "*Fat* Boy."

I blinked from the force of Joe's words. I let my bike fall. I gasped, I forgot to breathe. And before my bike hit the ground, I had a wiffle bat in my fists and was running at Joe, breathing again, screaming and crying. The sound and tears exploded from my face so suddenly you'd think my face had jumped into the future, skipping over the ten transitional expressions which usually transport a face from neutral into a screaming, tear-spraying fountain of hell.

I ran at him with the bat lifted high, giving him no time to escape on his bike. He abandoned it and took off on foot. He raced around the house. I followed. We circled the house again and again. And because it's shameful for a big brother to run from his little brother in fear, Joe made sure I knew fear had nothing to do with it. Every chance he got, he looked over his shoulder and laughed at me.

I can still remember his happy face and that laugh. I knew he could hurt me, of course, but to hurt me and then laugh so merrily at my attempts to hurt him back, that was something new, and it pushed me to new levels of anger. Usually, Mom would have intervened by now, not allowing the situation to become dangerous. But we were outside where running and screaming are allowed, things that oftentimes mean "someone's having fun out there." And if my war cries made Mom worry for a moment, the sound of Joe's laughter eased her mind. We were just playing a game, a harmless war game. Or tag with screaming, laughing, and a bat. No need to intervene.

As Joe ran on and laughed on, the thick skull of my anger slammed on, driving its head into the same old slam-polished wall in my chest, but harder and harder than ever before, until suddenly, the wall cracked. It gave. The next slam broke through into a vast cavern, pitch dark, empty, and infinite. You guessed it: I had discovered within myself the great Chamber of Hate, the place where anger is free to expand without end. There's nothing to slow it down in there, nothing to stop it. In the Chamber, the smallest cries echo into thunder. Tears become the flood of a god. Roar, and the darkness worships you. What a wonderful discovery. Mom was right: "Dan, the best things about people can only be found within."

I gave the Chamber a try. I thought a mean thought: *I hate him*. As soon as the thought went out, I realized the Chamber worked. I knew, because for the first time in my life, I not only *thought* I hated Joe; I hated him in fact. With the Chamber's help, I'd thought it and felt it and knew it was true: I had supped from the bloody goblet of Cain.

This is when my wiffle-bat plan changed.

When I'd started chasing Joe, the plan was vague. It was this: "I'll get him!" Nothing more. And I had no idea what getting him meant, not really. But then I did know, and what I knew scares me a little when I think about it from time to time, though it didn't scare me then. What did I know? I knew that if I caught him, I was going to hit him with the wiffle bat until he died. Beat him to death; that was the plan. And not a single cell inside me was against it.

A major hitch in the plan was that wiffle bats are terrible weapons. They're light-weight plastic, and they're bright yellow. These are hints from the manufacturer that they're not built for murder. Who kills someone with something yellow? Who kills with something so weightless? If I'd actually caught Joe, the wiffle bat beating would have lasted weeks, and even then, thirst and exposure would have killed him long before the bat.

But I wasn't thinking clearly. I was thinking *kill*. I really was, which unfortunately means I'm capable of murder. I know we're all capable, that the Chamber of Hate exists in every one of us, but unlike you, I put capable to the test and *tried* to kill.

Eventually, I gave up, stopped running, Joe disappeared around the corner of the house, and I found myself on the lawn alone.

I was starving for air, but I was sane again.

Also, I was changed.

I now possessed the Chamber of Hate, the place where you can walk in mad and walk out lethal. And I had a feeling once you locate the Chamber, break into it, and spend some time there, the door stays open.

Maybe Joe felt this too. Because he used "Fat Boy" less and less after that day. Maybe the butcher boy who raged from the measureless space I'd discovered made us both think twice about where we allowed our war to take us.

Maybe that boy made us alter our strategy: Let's take killing off the table, maybe. I won't kill you on the inside if you won't kill me. Agreed?

Agreed.

your doodles, memories, illustrations, story ideas...

**LESSON 20:**

# Grandparents Can, in Fact, Run. You Just Have to Get Them Mad Enough

Here's how to know you've grown up:

You stopped running.

Kids run whenever they get a chance. Grownups don't. Even though grownups own the world and could run all the time if they wanted to.

You don't see grownups running in graveyards or Walmart aisles or over to dead animals on the side of the road carrying a sharp stick. Never. In these situations (and all others) grownups walk.

I'm not talking about running for exercise, for rounding out the buttocks. I'm talking about running for fun. The fun is the running, and the running is the fun.

Go to a family reunion and you'll notice grownups acting like planets, their movements graceful, predictable, and seemingly slow while children zip around like liberated space trash, using the no-nonsense gravity of these ponderous aunts and uncles to slingshot their way to higher speeds.

Go to *my* family reunion and see me standing there, running nowhere, just another gas giant stuck in old patterns, helpless to escape the long cycles of life.

One of my nephews has witnessed this. I know because a few months ago, he asked me a telling question:

"Uncle Dan, can you run?"

He wasn't inviting me on a run. He was asking if I'm capable of running, if I have it in me to do better than a walk.

His question basically means I haven't run in front of the family in a decade. If it keeps going like this, by the time I'm a grandparent, I'll be like my grandparents: runners only in family lore.

For example,

- The time Grampa Fred ran to catch an evil dog who was flying through the air toward my father's face.

- The time Grandfather Edgar ran from a dead bear. He found it at the dump, full of trash and maggots. He ran to vomit in the privacy of the woods.

- The time Grammy Nancy ran to beat a mean pig with a board to stop it from murdering all the other pigs, as one does in Maine from time to time.

But wait, why isn't there a story about my fourth grandparent, the one called Grandmother Lucille? Because to make this list, you have to be a grandparent with a running story that took place before I was born. Grandmother Lucille didn't have one of those. I had to be born first and live seven or eight years before she got a running story of her own.

So, I was born. I made my grandparental runners list, which included the three, then I considered Grandmother Lucille. I could have asked her my nephew's question—"Grandmother, can you run?"—but I didn't need to. I already knew she couldn't. The fastest I'd seen her move was on the porch swing, and even then, *my* legs were the motor.

But then it happened: On the canvas of a perfectly forgettable day, she ran.

And I *saw*.

Mom and I were visiting. We each brought something for the visit: Mom brought talk. I brought my squirt gun. I squirted butterflies, bees, mailboxes, and I especially squirted my name in the dust while pretending I was peeing it. I did these things forever until I became fixated on shooting Grandmother's screen door.

The squirts looked fascinating on the screen, like dew on a spider's web. How could I ever stop? I was doing way more than making a watery mess inside the house: I was being an artist, one who had advanced in a leap beyond his peeing phase into a phase that truly had a chance of reaching people.

Just before I pulled the trigger on another bullseye, a patch of screen about the height of a grandmother's face,

Grandmother's face came into view, shadowy and with a mouth as tight as a coin slot.

"*No*," she said. "No more."

I lowered my gun and smiled to help her remember I was me, her beloved, and said, "Sorry."

She evaporated into the darkness of the house, and I continued staring at the screen, admiring my artificial dew that shone all around the dry bullseye, a look so captivating it made me forget or ignore my interaction with Grandmother. How do I know I forgot or ignored? Because in ten seconds or less I went right back to my squirt work.

I blasted the dry patch then found others. I blasted until, once again, she appeared.

This time, Grandmother was so angry her mouth had vanished completely, and she advanced beyond speech, pitching her words from her head directly into mine:

*I said, "**NO MORE!**"*

This helped me remember or acknowledge that she *had* said that, and I felt bad. Another smile from me, much weaker, and an honest but lame "I'm sorry."

Again, she dematerialized.

And though I did feel sorry, there was one more dry patch. I had painted the rest of the screen dark and drippy and as pretty as anything in nature, all but that last parched puzzle piece that was in desperate need of refreshment.

I think it's occasionally possible for children to be repeat offenders without malice. There are only so many things a child can hold in the mind at once, and a powerful desire, one that has become a need, an obsession, like throwing homemade spears at stop signs or trying to chew an entire pack of gum all at once and not suffocate, can take up all the space the mind has to offer. Obedience is out of the question. There's no room for it. You might as well command a child to tap their head and rub their stomach and not play in traffic at the same time. You ask too much.

All this to say, I was possibly innocent when I squirted that last thirsty patch of screen.

After the deed, I stood there smiling, adoring my work.

But not for long.

The despair that follows accomplishment had only just begun to set in when the screen door burst open and revealed Grandmother. She was all eyes, all teeth. She was wild.

And she was *running*.

Running at me.

Instead of screaming or escaping, I froze, which reveals that I'm crap in a crisis. I just stood there waiting for consequences like a fool. Grandmother reached me in three horribly fast steps, grabbed me by the shoulders, and just before she headbutted me into oblivion…

She hugged me.

That's all, folks.

She "pulled me into a hug," as they say, and she hugged me. She didn't scream in my ear "I *TOLD* you to stop!" She didn't take my squirt gun and crush it to pieces between our hug. She just hugged me. Not a bear hug or the hug of a python, but a kindly hug, warm and wonderful. Then, without a word, she let me go and went back into the house.

I stood there staring. I wasn't staring at the dripping screen, my masterpiece, but at the darkness beyond the screen, trying to pin down and understand the mystery I'd just experienced.

*Grandmother can't run... but she did. Grandmother should have punished me massively, brutally...but she didn't.*

*Do I even know her?*

I stared and stared, and the darkness grew. It expanded until it was the world and the future, a future world so full of surprises and unknowns that I felt like a stranger in it, and very small. But at least I was well-connected:

I was the grandson of Mystery herself.

A part of me is still standing at that screen door, staring into darkness, wondering, trying to make sense of Grandmother's run and the wonderful hug hiding at the end of her anger. The rest of me has gone on from that place, forever changed by it. Since that day, I've never needed to squirt a screen door again.

Though if doing so could give the gift of one more surprising hug like that from Grandmother Lucille, a hug full of all the warmth and rage of love, a hug with a running start, I'd do it in a heartbeat.

your doodles, memories, illustrations, story ideas…

# LESSON 21:

# You Shouldn't Kill Your Little Sister, Even if She'd Go Along With it Just to Be With You

Was I a good older brother or a bad one? If Meg claims I was bad, she has proof.

Once, I found out she liked a friend of mine. "I like *Josh*," she said. "Swear you'll never tell."

I swore.

Josh biked over for a visit a few days later. When the visit was over, as he was riding away and Meg and I were standing side-by-side on the lawn, waving, I wondered if I should break my promise. I didn't wonder very much; I was too busy shouting after Josh: "Hey, Josh! Meg *LIKES* YOU!"

She gasped. She wept. She went into shock and then into hiding.

Why did I do this? It's simple: I had something compelling to share, to shout. That's all. And though I'm sad this was the reason, I'm also thankful. Sad, because this kind of reasoning belongs to a thoughtless nut sack of a bastard. Thankful, because at least I wasn't a premeditating nut sack of a bastard, which is worse.

Another time, Joe and I completely forgot Meg's birthday. On the day itself, having been severely encouraged by Mom and Dad, we borrowed cash from them, biked down to Tobey's General Store, and came back with chips, Bubblicious bubble gum, and a can of soda for her—and teriyaki jerky for us, which we ate while giggling on the way home. To our shame, which we were too young to feel, Meg really loved our last-minute trash.

Then there was the time I stole her Happy Meal toy, a Miss Piggy figurine, and imprisoned it in a mason jar I'd filled to the brim with leeches.

"Watch," I said, holding up the jar. The blood suckers' green, dark green, and spotted bodies oozed all over each other, squelching and sliding. Their suction-cup mouths looked like wide-open blind eyes as they sucked on the glass for a way out.

"Gross!" said Meg, laughing, never suspecting she would soon, and very soon, be crying.

"Keep watching," I said.

She did. Finally, the leech bodies parted, and there was Miss Piggy's face. It came forward, nose to the glass. Piggy's open, smiling mouth resembled a scream in the vampiric context of the leeches, and when the worm curtain closed, burying Piggy once more, Meg's open mouth resembled a scream too, because she was screaming.

Or how about the time I led Meg into the woods to show her an old, abandoned water tower and forced her to climb it with me? It was well over a hundred feet tall, and you got to the top by a skinny, wiggly, rusty ladder bolted to one of the tower's lean legs.

We arrived at the site.

"Wow," she said.

"We're climbing it," I said.

She leaned back and back, looking up and up. I don't remember if she agreed to climb right away or if I scared her into agreement, using old standbys like, "There's a bear in the woods," or "The woods are full of perverts waiting for little girls to be alone on the ground, so you'd better climb." But I do remember looking down at her when we were way above the tree line and thinking, *This is so crazy! She's actually doing this! We could both die, but she could really die.*

Meg climbed to the top. The highest thing she'd ever climbed. A kid who couldn't do a pullup, couldn't hang from a pullup bar for more than ten seconds. No problem. She followed me into the sky, risked her life just to be with me, because I said so.

And there's my shame again.

However, if Meg claims I was a good brother, she has proof for that too.

Some of Meg's favorite games, she played with me. Three games stand out in my memory. One was called "Baby," another was "Torture," and the last was "Adventure." We played Baby inside on rainy and subzero days. Torture was for road trips. And Adventure was our outside-of-cars-and-houses game. The goal was to have adventures outside. Vague, I know, but kids were vague back then. There was no internet, barely any proof we existed; therefore, many of our activities, like our lives, were hazy.

Before I explain the games, I should mention dancing. In gym class, I'd learned a handful of swing dancing moves, and I tried them out on Meg. Using extreme force, I spun, twisted, and swung her. And though she often fell spinning and twisting to the floor, she always jumped up again and swung right back into the brutal machine of my dance.

We eventually danced so well we started showing off for Mom, Dad, and others. Everyone loved our moves, but no one loved them more than Grandmother Lucille. She requested our dance whenever she visited, and we danced as if Meg's life depended on it, spinning, twisting, swinging so fast our blood stuck to our outer walls, and if anyone fell, we fell like we were trying to die. Grandmother Lucille beamed for all of it, for the children blurring with speed, for the children's explosive falls and slidings across the floor. "Encore!" said her smile, so we picked ourselves up again and danced.

Back to the games:

## BABY

In the game called "Baby," I was the baby. I would wrap up in a blanket and lie on a couch or on the floor and demand to be soothed and served. Though I was a baby, I could speak very well. I demanded food, demanded story time, demanded medical attention for sudden illnesses and teething wounds. Meg would dash about, trying to put out my screech and whine fires, and when she finally got me to sleep, I would spring from sleep kicking, screaming, and blubbering about night terrors, and then, while in the throes of my dream delirium, I would attack her.

Sometimes, always, Meg would say, "Can *I* be baby this time?"

And I'd say, "No."
"Why not?"
"Because *I'm* baby."
"But I want a turn!"

Then I would sigh, remove the bottle from my mouth, take off my bonnet, un-swaddle myself, and walk away while Meg begged me to stop: "Please stop, I beg you! You're the baby, *you're* the baby, I don't care! COME BACK!" And slowly but surely, I would allow myself to be persuaded.

## TORTURE

On road trips, Meg brought stuffed animal friends to keep her company—Mr. Bear, for example—and I would ask, "Can I hold him?"

This question was the beginning of the game.

"I don't know," Meg would say. "What about what happened last time?"

Last time, I had punched Mr. Bear in the stomach and kidneys repeatedly and then pressed my thumbs into his eyes, temporarily blinding him.

"That was a long time ago," I said.

"It was yesterday."

"But I've done a lot of thinking since then, and I'm sorry. I'm very sorry, believe me."

Meg made Mr. Bear tremble with terror, but she also made him turn his head in my direction. Clearly, he was willing to hear me out.

Meg frowned. "I still don't know. You hurt him so bad."

"I really did, and for that reason, I *feel* so bad. I've been thinking about Mr. Bear and his hard time ever since that awful day yesterday. If only I could take it all back..."

Mr. Bear's trembling stopped. He tipped his head slightly as he gazed at me, assessing the danger, but I saw a beautiful shine in his eyes, the shine of his gradually renewing faith in my humanity.

"You promise you won't hurt him?" Meg said.

"I can't hurt him," I said, "because the person I was before, the person who *could* hurt a good man like Mr. Bear, that person is gone. *Forever*. I wouldn't even recognize that person if I saw him in the mirror."

Meg sighed and looked at Mr. Bear. "What do *you* think?"

Bear rubbed his chin thoughtfully as he thought. He looked at me again, at Meg again. Back at me. More thoughtful rubbing of the chin.

Joe broke his older brother indifference to sneak a peep from his side of the car, curious about what Mr. Bear would decide.

Finally, after more sorrowful begging from me and one more sigh from Meg, Mr. Bear nodded his head and said in his little voice, "Yes."

Then Meg handed him over.

I received him gently and cradled him like he was my own son. I whispered sweet things to him and more apologies while Meg watched us with an approving and matronly expression, proud of her brother's redemption. But another expression gradually took over: It was the look of a little sister waiting on the brink of something shocking and fun, the face people make while watching the wick of a firework burn.

Suddenly, after about a heavy handful of seconds, I transformed from a caring and repentant friend of Mr. Bear into a monster.

I began by beating him, pounding his head and tummy with my fists. Then I smashed his face against the window, his glassy eyes clicking with ear-ringing brightness, activating Dad—"STOP IT! YOU'LL BREAK THE WINDOW!!"—then I wrapped my hands around Mr. Bear's neck and squeeze until spit dripped from my mouth. Meg fought me through it all, of course, attempting to get him back, making Dad say, "Stop fighting!" "We're not fighting! We're playing!" "Well, your playing sounds like fighting, so *STOP IT!*" and while I tortured on, a little more quietly, Meg used arguments like, "You're killing him!" and "He'll never trust you again!" and "This is unforgivable!"

Eventually, I let Mr. Bear go, prompting Joe to look away again.

Meg took Mr. Bear back and held him as far away from me as possible, whispering comforts in his ears while he trembled and wept.

I did nothing to stop Meg's comforting. It was perfectly natural. My fault, even. I sat back and allowed Mr. Bear to go through the necessary stages of trauma recovery, and then, little by little, I began to show my grief and remorse. I groaned. I hung my head, put my face in my hands, and cried. "What have I done?" I said. "What kind of a monster am I?"

"The worst kind," Meg said.

"Yes, the worst. The *very* worst. If only I could... no. Never mind. I deserve prison and hard labor and the gas chamber."

"If only you could what?" Meg asked.

I glanced over and noticed Mr. Bear was looking at me again, and somehow—how could it be?—yes, somehow, he still had that shine in his eyes, the shine of hope. It was only the slightest shine, a mere glint, but real nonetheless, a shine saying, "Maybe, just maybe, this time will be different. Perhaps, though I fear to say it, and yet I must... perhaps it really is possible for a human being, for a *person*, to change. I have to believe it's possible, for what is life without possibility, without hope? I would gladly risk my life for hope."

Encouraged by this complex yet easily readable look of his, I began again making my case for the right to hold Mr. Bear. Meg offered counter arguments that inevitably weakened until she and Mr. Bear once again arrived at the moment of truth.

Meg looked at Mr. Bear. He looked at me. "No," Meg said, taking hold of his head, and turning it. "Look at *me*." She wiped her eyes. "This decision is about you. It's *yours*. You know what he's done, and you've heard what he has to say. Do you want to give him another chance? It's up to you. Whatever you decide is okay with me."

Mr. Bear thought and thought. He scratched his chin and thought some more. And while he thought and thought, the light of hope in his eyes grew brighter and brighter until finally he nodded his head and said in his little trusting voice, "Yes."

Poor bastard.

## ADVENTURE

Again, Adventure was about having adventures outside. I'll make this less vague with an example you already know:

Remember that time I led Meg into the woods and forced her to climb an old, abandoned water tower? Hundreds of feet tall, way above the treetops, a journey along a ladder that felt as trustworthy as a chain of insect skeletons?

Yeah, that time.

You remember how we arrived at the site, and Meg said, "Wow," and I said, "We're climbing it"?

She didn't want to, but I knew what it would mean to her, so I helped her want to by letting her know about all the bears and perverts in the woods.

"You don't want to be down here alone," I said. "Trust me."

And she did.

Meg took to the ladder after me and trusted my lead as we made our way into the sky.

When we broke through the treetops, I looked down and thought, *This is so crazy! She's actually doing this!*

*We could both die, she could* really *die, but she's climbing. SHE'S AMAZING!*

Meg reached the top. She stood with me on the highest height she'd ever climbed. No problem. After all, she was with me. I'd guided her, showed her the way. I had risked her life so she could be with me.

Because that's the kind of brother I am.

**LESSON 22:**

# A Kid Who Eats His Shoes Often Has a Pretty Good Reason

In elementary school, we played a game called "Steal the Bacon," and I was one of the all-time great bacon thieves.

Here's how it worked.

Two competitors stood at opposite ends of the gym. The bacon, a red rag, sizzled on the half-court line. When the gym teacher wasn't getting fired for inappropriate behavior, he blew the whistle, and the competitors raced for the bacon. Whoever grabbed it first and ran back to their starting line without getting tagged by the other kid was the champion.

That day in gym, I defeated Brandon, Tim, Jim, James, and Landon, and finally, it was time for me to race against the most exciting opponent of all:

O Henry

Henry the Smelly.

The Angry.

Henry the Legendary. For what? His amazing rage, his fantastic fits. O Henry, our Henry, professional tantrum man and maker of the everlasting memories.

During baseball season, in front of a crowd, I'd seen him strike out, hurl his helmet at teammates and coaches, then fall to the ground screaming, gnash his teeth to pieces, kick up dust, and tear his clothes to shreds like mad Old Testament prophets, pissed because God wouldn't kill some civilization that hurt their feelings, and so forth.

When Henry went shopping with his mother, if he wanted a toy but she said, "No," he'd turn himself into a hurricane, wrecking the store until she caved.

It was the same at school. When he lost footraces or got tagged in games of tag or someone hit him with a snowball in a snowball war he'd started, he produced a thrilling outburst. All Henry's outbursts were thrilling, extremely entertaining events, especially if you weren't his coach, his teachers, or his mother.

I was none of these.

I was the undefeated thief of bacon, and I was about to help Henry the Smelly perform his wrath act in front of the entire third grade.

Yes, he smelled. Always like sweat. Sometimes like gasoline. Often like spit: He daily chewed on the collars of his shirts until he'd made a stain the shape of a Canadian province over his entire chest.

In other words, success in the third grade meant one thing: Whatever you do, *DON'T BE HENRY.*

He and I took our positions for the race.

Toes to the lines. My toes were housed in either Converse or Converse, shoes badly abused by asphalt, gravel, and muck, but they were in top-notch condition compared to Henry's.

For one, his shoes reeked, a smell you'd expect from the shoes of Lazarus when he sauntered out of the tomb, resurrected, flyblown, damp, and drippy.

For two, Henry's shoes looked *awful.*

They were old and tattered, held together in part by shoelaces of many colors—a thousand fragments of molting string tied together. The laces looked like stitches stretched to bursting on the body of a water-bloated corpse. There were parts of Henry's shoes the laces couldn't help, and these were secured by duct tape, so much duct tape, it wrapped his shoes like tape around a boxer's fists, a boxer found dead at the bottom of the lake come spring.

I paid close attention to Henry's smells and clothes, but did I wonder what it felt like to smell bad all the time and wear the shoes of the dead? Did I wonder why he smelled, why he dressed in ruins every day, or why he raged and threw tantrums, something the rest of us did, yes, but only in the privacy of our homes, like men?

I did not.

Mostly what I did was carry close to my heart the magnificent knowledge that Henry the Legendary went mad if you pushed the right buttons. And I was about to push those buttons. In front of everyone, I would steal the bacon from Henry, no sweat.

I was excited. *What's he gonna do?* I was nervous. *What's he gonna **do?*** But nervousness was normal. Part of what made Henry's show entertaining was that it was frightening.

Was I a horrible kid?

Should I have held back and let him win?

It would have been very big of me to do this, to lose when I so badly wanted to see what losing would do to him. To give this up, doing so in front of friends who would punish me, that would have been very big of me indeed. Also, it would have been impossible. There was too much pressure—the people wanted their entertainment—but more significantly, I wasn't a kid who held back, not for anything or anyone. If I could beat you, I beat you. Connect Four, Guess Who?, Go Fish, I beat you. Battleship, dodgeball, kickball, I killed you. Ping pong, I located you in hell and ate your spirit. And I especially ate your spirit when it came to Steal the Bacon. Listen, even if Steal the Bacon was something you'd requested in the place of your last meal before your execution, I would make sure you met your maker as a loser.

Henry and I stood on our lines, crouching down, waiting for the whistle. *Ready.* Eyes on the bacon.

My buddies whispered encouraging things to me like "Get him" and "Destroy Henry," and though I was about to—nothing on Earth would stop me, least of all Henry—he looked determined, even hopeful.

The hell?

Did he think he could win? Did he not understand that he was Henry and I was me?

The gym teacher put the whistle to his unnervingly moist and glistening lips, drew in a breath of pungent third-grade air, then blew a scream from the whistle's mouth.

Henry and I were off.

Our sneakers screeched, we bared our teeth, our hearts and eyeballs bulged, meaty grenades shivering to explode. We gave everything we had to win, and though the stakes were high for me—if Henry won, I'd be a loser for a day or two—the stakes were super high for Henry. If he lost, he'd be a boy screaming and crying in front of everyone. I wonder if he knew this. Did he know losing would absolutely make him do something humiliating? Or were his rages surprises, as shocking to him as they were to everyone else? If they weren't a surprise, if he *did* know what would happen after a loss, then he was running not only to win, but to save himself from another social catastrophe, and that was the reason for his determination. But what explained his ridiculous hope?

Nothing could. But this is the nature of hope.

We ran toward that bacon. On and on, we ran, boiling our blood to send us faster toward an unknown, even though I knew:

*I'm going to win.*

I don't remember if I discovered the whole truth about Henry before or after our bacon race. I hope it was after. If it was before, then I have to wonder: Where was my sympathy, empathy, and compassion? And what does it mean that I still don't know the difference between these words?

The big discovery about Henry took place on a church workday, a Saturday, my most sacred day. Mom and Dad forced Joe and me to join the work crew. The plan was to cut, split, and stack firewood for Henry's mother. Unfortunately, no one knew the stove's dimensions, so the chainsaw people didn't know how long the firewood needed to be. Someone had to get those dimensions. To do that, someone had to knock on the door and ask.

But everyone thought it would be awkward to knock and ask, because it seemed the family—Henry, his sister, and their mother—didn't want to be disturbed. What gave this impression? The closed curtains, the broken steps, the waist-high grass, the leprous paint, the sagging roof, and the fact that the family was home, their car was there, and yet no one had rushed out to praise us or pay us for throwing away our Saturday.

Since no volunteer volunteered to disturb the family, an angry deacon made me and Joe do it. He armed us with a tape-measure then ordered us to knock.

We navigated the tall grass, the trash in the grass—broken mowers and car parts—and approached the broken steps. We moved slowly, as if the house was the temple of a dangerous god.

We climbed the rot-soft steps, looked at each other, then we knocked.

No answer.

Not from people anyway. The answer we got was the shouting of what sounded like 170 small dogs.

We knocked again. Louder. Longer.

Nothing.

Then the gigantic red face of the angry deacon materialized above and behind us to say, "Just go in."

So, we tried the doorknob.

It was unlocked.

In we went.

And what we found, I'll never forget.

I hadn't heard of hoarding, but if I had, I would have imagined a collection of useful items: hills of TVs and VHS tapes, slopes of board games, mountains of comic books, candy, and action figures. But that's not what Henry's mother collected.

As far as Joe and I could tell, she collected garbage.

The moment we opened the door, we smelled it, and I thought of Henry. Here was his signature scent, though much, *much* stronger.

Garbage was everywhere.

Hills, slopes, and mountains of cardboard, junk mail, newspapers, books and broken books, pizza boxes, bottles, cans, plastic bags, decomposing clothes. A bathroom without a door revealed a yellowish toilet missing its seat and lid. A couch lay on its back, a line of howling dogs perched on top. The rest swarmed at our feet. And though it wasn't the dogs' fault, they were the ones who'd added gallons of shit and piss to the piles, hopefully the only ones. Stalactites of fly tape hung from the ceiling, but the tape's sticky yellow was completely gone, covered in flies, turning the tape into monstrous sticks of black rock candy. I couldn't see the floor anywhere. Garbage buried every inch and banked up the walls. Enormous blankets had been thrown over the trash to create a more walkable floor, but these too had begun to disappear, to sink beneath the awful collection.

And, again, the smell.

Not just rot, but a living rot, rot with a will. It scared us. We felt like we'd stumbled into

the nest of something cruel and lethal, something watching our every move, eager to bury and digest us beneath the years of mounded misery.

We stood frozen in the middle of it all, dead silent. We glanced at each other, passing shock and horror back and forth until we remembered the angry deacon and our mission. We measured the woodstove then got the hell out of there.

What happened after is a blur. We told our disturbing story, and in the following weeks, the church went in and saw what we had seen. People started whispering about the amazing number of trash bags the workers filled. 50 bags. Enormous bags. 100. 200. 500 bags of pure trash. Impossible, but true.

What's come to bother me more than the smell and the garbage and even the heartbreaking lives of the dogs is that Joe and I hadn't seen Henry or his family in the house, though we knew they were there.

Where had they been?

We had no choice but to imagine.

They must have heard the unthinkable—knocking on the door—and then the even more unthinkable: a turning doorknob, and the front door creaking open. That's when they must have dashed away to conceal themselves beneath the garbage until we were gone.

Henry under trash. Hiding. His sister too. And their mother. A grown woman breathing shallowly to keep the trash above her from rustling and giving away her position. She could do this very well, and she'd passed the skill on to her children. They were pros. Here was a family so good at concealment and silence I wonder if even the dogs lost track of them now and then. And maybe the family members occasionally dug in and hid from each other. I picture Henry hunting high and low for his mother and then finally giving up and settling in to wait until she resurrected in her own good time.

Did I feel sympathy, empathy, or compassion after seeing Henry's house?

I felt disgust, dread, amazement, fascination, and awe. Does that count?

But why didn't I feel for him? It wasn't because I refused to or was incapable of that kind of emotion. It just didn't occur to me. I would have felt bad for myself if I was in his place, but I wasn't. He was. Because he was Henry, and I was me. And what was I?

Anything (oh, yes, *anything*) but Henry.

Again, before or after the trash revelation, Mr. Gym Teacher's whistle blew. Henry and I ran for bacon. His eyes were huge, crazy with that hope of his. Every tooth in his head showed itself, and his teeth were locked together tightly as a dungeon door, tightly as if he hung over hell by a rope in his teeth. That kind of intensity, friends, is hard to beat.

Unless you're so much faster.

I got to the bacon first, easily. I snatched it up, pivoted fast, then ran back, knowing Henry was right behind me, chasing, losing all the way to my victory line.

But I was wrong.

He wasn't behind me.

After winning, I turned around and saw that Henry had returned to his own line some time ago. Everyone stood at a distance from him, and everyone stared. Because Henry was sitting on the floor; Henry was lifting one of his sneakered feet to his mouth; Henry was ferociously tearing at the duct tape with his teeth. Eating it. Or maybe not, but it looked enough like he was eating it, that's how I'll always remember it. In the years to come, people would even claim they'd seen Henry eat both of his shoes *whole*, down to the laces, and then slurp them up like spaghetti.

Everyone watched.

Awestruck.

Fascinated.

Amazed.

Full of dread.

Disgusted.

Thoroughly entertained.

The whistle dropped from the gym teacher's mouth. The children's mouths hung open, some half smiling, others rounded in wonder. And on and on, Henry tore away at those ruined shoes. Screaming, shredding, lunging for more.

He was a sight and sound filling the gym to the top. He was a kid with a rage that knocked him right out of his shoes, a boy who lived every day and night in a giant box of trash.

He was Henry.

And I was me, a boy reduced to a pair of terrified, delighted eyes, hovering a short distance above the finish line, enjoying my win.

your doodles, memories, illustrations, story ideas...

# LESSON 23:

# The Road to Heaven May Be Rough, But it Isn't Hell

You guessed it: In elementary school, I was in a gang.

We didn't beat people up, graffiti stuff, or sell drugs. We were a Christian gang, which means our gang activities came down to discussing hell amongst ourselves for fun and discussing hell with unbelievers to scare them into heaven. For glory. If you were unsaved and in our way, we talked to you about hell and didn't stop until you fled from us or fled with us, straight to Jesus.

One year, a new girl came to school. Amelia MacArthur. I thought Amelia was interesting because her family lived in a big old farmhouse that looked like it had been built by ghosts:

- roofs sagging like smiles
- windows black as dead pupils, staring windows
- bone-white paint covering the whole thing like the house was a long and lumpy giant wrapped in a sheet to play a Halloween ghost, or a dead giant in a winding sheet

Also, Amelia told me a wonderful story about the house. She said the farmers' daughter died long ago and for some reason they buried her beneath one of the walkway flagstones leading to the front door.

I thought about that dead girl: lying in the dirt, her white dress glowing like a grub, her eyes open, her smile bristling with the pale roots of weeds. I imagined you would know which flagstone was hers because you'd feel coldness seeping into your feet, climbing the marrow tunnels of your bones higher and higher, and if you stood there too long, the cold would hit your heart like snake poison, and you, like a little farm girl yourself, would drop dead.

I declared Amelia my friend.

My Christian gangmates liked her too, or they liked that she was new and might join our gang. We only had to learn where her soul was headed after death: into the fun or into the fire.

I don't remember how, but we found out Amelia did not believe in God. So, it was fire.

We cracked our knuckles and necks like holy fighters and the sound said, "She doesn't believe in God… *yet.*"

The gang found her in the library sitting alone at a long table, drawing farm animals and dead farm children. We advanced. One by one, we filled the chairs around the table. With every blink, another Christian appeared. Soon, we were all there.

"Hello, Amelia," we said. We didn't say it like that, eerily and in unison, but we might as well have.

"Hi," said Amelia, surrounded but unfazed. She must have thought that we, her friends, were there to be friendly. And we were. We were there to be friendly to Amelia's *soul* by scaring the crap out of it. Saving it.

We asked her, "What are you drawing?"

"Just farm stuff." She started pointing, labeling her work: "Here's the cow, the pig, the dead kids. Here's a goat, but he isn't finished—"

"We heard you don't believe in God."

She looked at us and blinked. "What?"

Fair question.

We answered with another question: "Do you know where you're going when you die? Heaven or *hell*?"

A worried look took over her face, but not nearly worried enough. Why wasn't she trembling, crying? Clearly, she hadn't done any serious thinking about death.

And now, we hit her with the biggest question of all: "Do you believe in Jesus?"

"Yes," she said.

A very surprising answer. For a moment, we didn't know what to do. Was our intel bad? Did she, in fact, believe? If so, our intervention was unnecessary, and we'd have to transition into a fun and friendly gang initiation ceremony, which is difficult after you've group stared at a person and semi-casually brought up their death.

But on second thought, there was something a little troubling about her answer, that offhanded "yes" of hers. Something too light and breezy about it, too easy. And now she was drawing again. This made her seem insincere. There's something deceitful about a person who declares their allegiance to Jesus and then goes right back to drafting a goat.

"So, you believe in him?" we said.

"Yes."

"What do you mean?"

"What do you mean what do I mean?"

She had us there. Panic flashed in our eyes. We rallied: "You believe in him... but *how* do you believe in him?"

"How?"

"Yeah, how?" Then one of us, we might as well call him Christian, figured out how to say it: "You believe in Jesus, but do you believe Jesus was God?"

"*Is* God," we corrected, "not *was* God. *IS*."

Christian winced, started sweating, then tried again: "Do you believe Jesus *is* God?"

Amelia thought about it briefly then said, "My sister told me he was just a man. I guess that's what I think."

And there it was. We'd gathered good intel after all, which was fortunate for our informants and very fortunate for Amelia; she was about to be saved.

After hearing her confession, my friends possibly tried to remember Bible verses about God's love to use against her. I didn't try that because I didn't know verses. I knew Bible stories, especially the violent ones, because they made me laugh. The rock sinking into Goliath's forehead like a thumb into dough. The fat king's belly swallowing Ehud's knife. Jael pounding a tent peg into the head of a sleeping camper.

And my favorite of all: the "she bears."

Here's the story. A bunch of ancient children teased the prophet Elisha until he decided: *Enough is enough*:

"He turned around, looked at them and called down a curse on them in the name of the Lord. Then two she bears came out of the woods and mauled forty-two of the children," 2 Kings 2:24.

"She bears" is hilarious. That in combination with the fact that they half murdered a bunch of asshole children made it comedy gold. At weddings and funerals, I'd challenge myself by flipping through the Bible until I found the story, then I'd fight against laughter so hard I'd just about implode.

I didn't share my she bears with Amelia or any other tale of carnage that day, and no one in the gang recited love verses. To be honest, no one tried. Those weren't the verses we knew anyway.

What did we know?

We knew hell.

Christian brought it up: "Guess what happens if you don't believe Jesus is God? Ever heard of the Lake of Fire? No? Okay, so imagine a lake. Now imagine it's on *fire*, got it?" The rest of us got it, easily—we were always imagining it—then we merrily joined Christian in giving Amelia visions of damnation. We told her about the lake's unquenchable fire, about the worms in the burning water, the ones who dieth not. "It means they never die," we said, "and neither does anyone or anything else. You'll wanna die, but you can't. There's no way out of the *pain*. Listen, have you ever burned yourself?"

Amelia nodded.

"Imagine that feeling all over your body. *Forever!*"

We shared with her the weeping, the gnashing teeth, and the unimaginably heavy loneliness. All without breaking a sweat.

Then we flexed.

Not only had we paid attention in church whenever hell came up, we'd been inventing hells of our own for most of our lives, coming up with newer, bigger, badder versions, outdoing one another with more exquisite tortures. Each of us had at least 10 hells. As we shared them, some of our ideas overlapped, but repetition is a big part of learning in elementary school.

Amelia, a good student, paid close attention and continued to learn.

She learned about hell's washing machines, the "people washers," machines full of knives and saltwater. She learned about tumors that grow all over your body, growing and bursting and regrowing as fast as boiling water. She learned about the carnivorous creatures that look exactly like the people you love most, people you're dying to see again—you miss so much—but when you get too close, they pin you down with their powerful arms and bite you over and over, trying to eat you, until you can get away, if you can ever get away.

"So, it's your *sister* who eats you alive!" Christian said. "Or your grandma, or your *mom*."

On and on we went, delightedly assaulting the walls of Amelia's unbelief. Eventually, I think we forgot why we were telling her so much about hell and simply enjoyed showing off our nightmares before a new audience. And what an audience. We watched Amelia's face turn pale and her eyes go wide, filling with tears as our images bloomed in her brain; we watched her shrink in her seat and then sit so still you'd think she was playing dead, as if she'd found herself in a lair of she bears and the only way out was to bore them with death.

Not a bad plan, as she bears don't care about death at all. They care about suffering.

When we paused to catch our breath, Amelia asked in a tiny voice how we knew these things about hell. How could we possibly know? We answered by telling her other things about hell. We talked so fast, validating each other's inventions and hell facts with head nods and thumbs up; we constantly interrupted one another, adding to each other's hells, creating something new before Amelia's eyes, the words switching from mouth to mouth, making it difficult for her to know where to look. Which face was talking about the acid pools, the anus leeches, the backwards knee machine? It was this face, that face, the one right beside her. *All* the faces. She closed her eyes for a moment, but our voices found her there. Her eyes opened. Her *mind* opened to the horrible possibility we were sharing and building, a possibility that seemed more and more likely as we talked on and on, our words a whirlwind, a whirlpool in the lake of fire, pulling Amelia down and down until it happened....

She burst into tears.

We shut our mouths. Our teeth snapped together, imprisoning our busy tongues. We stared at her and at each other, shocked. Had our hells been *that* good, that scary? The answer was yes, but we didn't know. How could we? Hell isn't scary for people who never have to go there. People like that can afford to turn the place into a game, anything to pass the eternity of sitting through a Sunday morning sermon.

Amelia cried on. We watched, wide-eyed and terrified. We glanced at the librarian, wondering if she would notice Amelia and punish us. If you make a kid cry hard, you get in trouble. We didn't like trouble. I especially didn't like it. I feared it above all things. One harsh word from an adult, even if I'd earned it, reduced me to the dirt behind my ears.

We hurdled over our shock and tried to comfort Amelia, to quiet her, and we continued peeking at the librarian. But she didn't seem to notice the crying. Maybe she was a hardened veteran when it came to children's suffering and would have only responded if we'd set Amelia on fire, which we'd tried our best to do.

"Sorry, Amelia!" we said. She kept crying. So, we added, "We didn't mean to scare you!" This wasn't true, of course. Scaring her had been the point. She cried on.

But then we had an idea. We remembered why we'd been telling her about hell in the first place.

"Amelia, *listen*," we said, "all you have to do is believe Jesus is God then ask him into your heart. Ask forgiveness for your sins, and you'll be saved. You'll get to go to heaven! You won't have to go to hell, not ever!"

We said it over and over—"You don't have to go to hell!"—until gradually Amelia's crying stopped. She listened to our words, nodding now and then, sighing, wiping her eyes. It seemed she was hearing us, deeply. Possibly believing. We watched her so carefully, unblinking, holding our breaths. Was this really happening? Was she about to say the magic words so we could go home and yell at our parents, "I did it! I saved someone today!"?

Mom and Dad would cheer for me. If they asked how I went about delivering the good news of salvation to Amelia, I would possibly avert my eyes as I said, "I just... told her the truth." Then I'd rally: "She even cried!"

Amelia wiped her nose and eyes and looked around at us, her friends. Then she did it. She prayed the prayer, the "sinner's prayer," the ticket out of hell forever.

Did we cheer? I don't remember. Did we tell our parents and grandparents and make the announcement at church and receive praise? Definitely. Did Amelia's salvation immediately grant her membership into our gang? Not really. I think Amelia remained mostly a free agent at our little country school. There are always kids like her, the ones who never quite fit. But that didn't matter to us. She was saved. Even if this world rejected her, even if we did, Jesus would catch her in the end.

After Amelia said "amen," she asked a question:

"What's it like?"

We didn't understand. We'd already told her. "We already told you. It's horrible: fire, worms, leg-breakers, etc. Weren't you listening?"

"No, I mean, what's heaven like?"

We said nothing for a moment or two. We glanced at each other then down at our hands as we tried to think of an answer. Our silence made the librarian look at us. Christian smiled and waved. The librarian looked away again. I considered telling Amelia that heaven is where the dead farm girl went and waited for her parents—it's a place of reunion and love—but that would have taken the wonderful ghost out of the ground, a ghost I wanted to keep right where she was.

When our silence became too embarrassing for us to bear, we tossed out a few images. What's heaven like? It's clouds. A gate. People in robes. Angels. Lots of light. Gold. God. Then we fell back into silence. What could we say about heaven?

Anything else?

Nothing?

Honestly, we'd never really thought about it.

**LESSON 24:**

# Teachers Have Emotions Too, and Pasts, and Were Once Young, and Can Feel Pain

In seventh grade we had a long-term substitute teacher who was a hunchback. That's the word we used. Being seventh graders, we liked our words from the 18th century, especially if this added that extra punch of cruelty.

I've been a sub. It's a tough job even with the best of spines. Even if you've won spine pageants, being a sub sucks. You're the rent-a-cop of the classroom, the stepparent who joined the family too soon after Mom ran off or died off, and we hate your clothes, your voice, your authority, and your face. We will defy you—we must—or die trying, though we'd prefer that you do the dying.

It also sucks having kyphosis, "a condition in which the spine in the upper back has an excessive curvature." A condition that could happen to any of us, even seventh graders, but we didn't know that.

Yes, Mrs. Daigle had kyphosis, but that wasn't the problem.

She was also the oldest teacher we'd ever seen. I'm not going to say I found out later she was only fifty-five, and isn't it amazing how the definition of "old" changes as you get old? This is true, but it's not her story. Mrs. Daigle was in her upper eighties. She'd returned from retirement to do the school a favor in a pinch, and the pinch lasted longer than expected.

But her age wasn't the problem either.

The problem was her meanness. She was mean. Which meant we hated her and made fun of her constantly. What did we use for material? I'd be a liar if I said kyphosis and age didn't come up from time to time.

## Mrs. Daigle's Meanness

She said things like "quiet" during our study hall.

We didn't like that.

We didn't understand it. If she'd done her research, she would have learned that, historically, study halls are for talking and having fun.

One day, after Mrs. Daigle told us to be quiet a dozen times, one of us, a bold captain of the group, said, "But all the other teachers let us talk in study hall." Suddenly, Mrs. Daigle slammed her fist down and thundered a statement we would repeat thousands of times:

"Well, you're in *my* study hall now!"

It just sounded so epic. From a movie, a horror movie. Therefore, from then on, we slammed our fists on everything—desks, walls, each other—hunched our backs, and delivered the line, "You're in **MY** study hall now!" adding mad laughter, "HahaHahahahHA!" and it always got us roaring.

Also, she constantly compared students to this perfect grandson of hers. She used him as an example of how we should behave, and she quoted him often, especially his most famous line:

"I like it *quiet.*"

She explained that she, like her grandson, also liked it quiet, and that we should be less like ourselves and more like her and her pristine, de-balled grandson. And when she said his famous line, she drew out the "quiet" to the point that she almost sang the word.

"I like it qu*iiiiii*et."

We added this to our behind-her-hunchback act and used it whenever we could.

She did any number of other mean things, like expecting us to work, expecting us to listen in class, expecting us to recognize her humanity, so we had no choice…

We pushed back even harder.

## One: Shit

One time, a kid named Pete swore at Mrs. Daigle to her face. He assumed what we all assumed, that she was hard of hearing.

He raised his hand, and she said, "Yes?" and he said, a little softly, "I gotta go take a shit."

Mrs. Daigle nodded and said, "Go ahead," and the rest of us convulsed dangerously with suppressed amazement and delight.

A wonderful thing had happened, but it was also very confusing. Mrs. Daigle had heard Pete's statement well enough to let him use the bathroom, but poorly enough that she'd missed his "shit." But if she *had* missed his shit, how did she know he needed a bathroom break? So, she hadn't missed it—she wasn't hard of hearing at all. However, if this is true, why didn't she punish Pete for his shit?

Today, thirty years later, I still don't understand it.

Though maybe we were right, and she did have trouble hearing, so when Pete said, "I gotta go take a shit," she thought he said, "I, like my fellow classmates, am a real piece of shit. Show me that you agree by allowing me to shed some of my shit in the restroom."

"Go ahead."

## Two: Burn It

James was a bad kid. He'd push Mrs. Daigle's buttons until she sent him to the principal's office. Which is exactly what he wanted. The principal was his father.

Once James departed, the fun would begin.

The classroom had two doors, and James would use them both. After leaving, he'd stand in the hall and count to 100, about the time it took to walk to the office, then we'd see a mischievous hand slip around the doorframe into the room and hit the lights.

In the sudden dimness, Mrs. Daigle would look up at the killed lights, and James would race down the hall to the other door. The moment Daigle tried the light switch, turning the lights back on, James would hook his hand through the other door and switch them off again. Over and over, as long as he could keep it going.

Once, while Mrs. Daigle's back was turned, James reached into the classroom, grabbed the American flag, which was standing nearby and yet untarnished, and waved it up and down violently. When Mrs. Daigle felt a disturbance in the union and turned, James dropped the flag on the floor and ran.

And *she* ran.

Or walked briskly. But to us, she ran. She was an eighty-nine-year-old hunchback. She *sprinted*. She spread her veiny leather wings and flew. And at the door, she shouted, "James! *James!*"

This became another catchphrase of ours. We'd see a friend. When the friend said "Hey" or "What's up?" or "What's the homework?" we'd say, "James! *JAMES!!!*" and everyone would laugh like people drunk on love.

## Three: The Day Of The Great Shock

It must have been right before a break. Maybe summer break. That was the size of the energy inside us. And an ugly energy. Group evil, the kind that makes strangers in musicals bump into each other and sing the exact same song, *perfectly*, which is nothing if not demonic; the kind of evil that makes lemmings leap from cliffs.

**FATHER LEMMING**: If your friends told you to jump off a cliff, would you?

**CHILD LEMMING**: Yes.

**FATHER LEMMING**: And it wouldn't be your fault, son. No one could resist that.

That day of ugly energy, of evil, we, the seventh graders, decided to give Mrs. Daigle a shock.

## Time to Get Technical

I misled you before when I said the classroom had two doors. In addition to the two leading into the hallway, there were two others. These two connected our room to classrooms on either end. One of these classrooms was not in use, and it was the one with the door directly behind Mrs. Daigle's big desk.

## Time to Get Evil

When class began, Daigle noticed a problem right away.

We were not there.

Picture Mrs. Daigle. She's sitting at her desk. She's glancing at the clock, at all the empty seats. Imagine her wondering what's going on. Imagine her thinking what I would be thinking if I was her: *Maybe they were all caught performing elder abuse somewhere and are now on their way to juvie, praise God.*

Right after she thought this, the door at her back flew open, and we burst into the room, leaping and howling and wiggling and dancing.

That was the whole plan. Burst through and party our way to our seats. Mrs. Daigle didn't seem overly shocked, which was good; in our ignorance, we hadn't considered the possibility that overly shocking a heart in its near nineties might be something close to murder.

You're disappointed, I know. After my build up, you expected big evil.

Wait for it.

Introducing Matt: He was a tall, goofy, frighteningly unpredictable kid, a kid who did something extra, something outside of the plan.

After everyone but Matt rushed through the door and passed Mrs. Daigle, who watched us boogie-woogie to our desks, Matt snuck up behind her. He'd been struck by inspiration. He grabbed the light sweater she often hung on the back of her chair. He swung it over the top of her head like he was helping her put on a necklace, then he pulled it back against her face.

Correct, it was an act of blinding, of smothering. To be fair to Matt, though, he didn't pull the sweater hard. It was a gentle blinding, a conscientious smothering, and for Matt, this was a triumph of goodwill.

Mrs. Daigle didn't see it that way.

She turned in time to spot him running and sped after him, shouting, "Matt! Matt! *Matt!*"

We added "Matt! Matt! MATT!!!" to our little book of comedy, though I don't remember us using it as much as we used the other gems.

Maybe because we realized we'd gone slightly too far. Maybe. Matt had at least. To our credit, we knew that much.

He should have been expelled, sued, and whatever else the law allows. We probably all should have been expelled. At least suspended. Our dancing flash mob must have felt like an attack. But believe it or not, I don't remember Mrs. Daigle ever calling for a punishment higher than detention. Even for Matt.

I don't know why.

Maybe because she was merciful. Maybe because our behavior, which we thought was so badassed, was nothing compared to what Mrs. Daigle had seen in her time. Maybe she thought, *I don't want you expelled. I want you here so I can break you with my bare hands.*

After the incident, we cooled it for a while, lying low, waiting for the dust to settle, and in that window of relative peace, Mrs. Daigle gave *us* a shock.

I don't remember why she brought in photographs from home. Maybe she was dragging us through a unit on family history.

Of the photos she brought, I only remember one.

It was a big, framed picture of Mrs. Daigle on her wedding day. It was a black and white photograph of her standing beside a little table covered in gifts. She was with a young man, her husband, and she was young. And tall, without the slightest bend in her back, and her hair was long and shining, she was smiling, and I remember thinking, *Wow*.

I remember all of us thinking it.

A complicated thought we didn't understand. Because we were young and cruel and worshiped at the Church of Youth. But I think I can break down this thought of ours now.

*Wow, you were once young! Why didn't you tell us?!*

*Wow, you and that guy look like movie stars! You should have mentioned there was a time when you were interesting!*

*Wow, I never would have had a shot with you! Is your perfect grandson hot and single? Do you have perfect granddaughters too? I could learn to like it quiet.*

*Wow. What is this foreign feeling growing in my chest? Regret? Am I suddenly wishing I could take everything back? To be fair to me, though, I just had no idea you used to be someone. None of us did.*

*Wow.*

*Why didn't you tell us you were beautiful?*

your doodles, memories, illustrations, story ideas...

**LESSON 25:**

# If You Want to Meet an Axe Murderer, Look No Further Than the Boy Next Door

There's a tree in Maine that bears the following words:
"Phil And Phil"

One of the Phils stands for my middle name, which is Philip. The other Phil stands for Phil, the little brother of James, who was my brother's best friend in those days.

"I have an idea," people said. "You younger brothers should be friends too." Obviously, people said this because of our older brothers' friendship and because of the Phil thing.

"Listen, people," I said, "shouldn't friendships be based on more than coincidences?"

"No," said the people. "This is a small town and broke. Coincidences are all we have for you. Be grateful."

So, Phil and I tried friendship. We started off big by turning ourselves into a club:

The Phil-and-Phil

Though Phil was younger and smaller than me, he shrewdly rose to my level, liking the things I liked:

- *Raiders of the Lost Ark*
- Monsters
- *Indiana Jones and the Temple of Doom*
- Pyramids
- *Indiana Jones and the Last Crusade*
- Ninjas
- Hats
- Whips
- Fast women
- Big League Chew

And where I'd only seen the TV version of *The Temple of Doom*, the version in which they edited out the doom part—the guy ripping the other guy's heart out using only passion, his hand, and a powerful denial of the existence of ribs—Phil had seen the unmolested version.

He described the heart scene in detail, putting the doom back in, which the movie needed. Otherwise, it was just a bunch of kids working all day for someone else's reasons: *The Temple of School*.

"Amazing," I said, "but did it look *real*?"

"*So* real," said Phil, in that voice of his, a whispery, faraway voice, the voice of a boy's ghost squatting at the bottom of a well, a ghost who just won the coincidence jackpot in the form of a brand-new friendship, and he knows it.

Phil and I decided heart ripping was real and talked about it forever. We also discussed arks, bigfoots, ribless torsos, mummies, Sean Connery, the delightful meanings of the word ninja ("one who is invisible" and "one who sneaks"), the appropriateness of fedoras in our time, air travel by whip, and women with hungry arms.

Yes, we discussed it all, a thing that should have been impossible with the morbidly impressive payloads of grape-flavored chaw in our mouths.

Sitting in that old clubhouse, which was just a lean-to against the Phil-And-Phil tree, I thought, *This is nice, being in the woods with a friend. Phil's a cool guy. I wonder why James ignores him and faithfully leaves him out of everything.*

Now you know: James left Phil out. Of *everything*.

But why?

I looked at Phil, who with concentration and patience that were beyond his years and my years put together, was carving our names deeper into the tree, and I shrugged. *I have no idea why James ignores Phil and faithfully leaves him out of everything. Oh well. James's loss is my gain.*

*Phil-and-Phil forever.*

The next day, we went to our fort again. More of the same talk. We talked about the depressingly inaccessible warehouse-sized reliquaries controlled by our overreaching Executive Branch; the sad fact that crusades were over. You can't have another one after you find out they've already had the last one; and the even sadder fact that in real life we'd seen as many fast women as we'd seen spontaneous heart extractions:

None.

We began to doubt their existence. And if they're not real, what is?

It was the same talk the next day.

And the next.

I didn't want to go anymore.

- It wasn't fun just sitting there with Phil staring at me unblinking as we talked about whatever I wanted to talk about instead of going out and doing things, having adventures.

- He didn't want to do things or have adventures.
- He wanted to sit right there, talking.
- *Forever.*
- Never coming up with anything of his own to talk about but pulling more and more out of me until I began to realize my fascination with myself might actually have limits.

Though when Phil occasionally did bring up something to talk about, it was always in the form of an interrogation.

He needed to know just how dedicated I was to Club Phil-and-Phil.

He'd throw scenarios my way:

- Would I still come to club meetings in a blizzard?
- In a flood?
- In the chaos following the collapse of Maine and America?
- What if Phil the younger suffered a terrible accident and lost his body but had his head rescued by science?
- Would I carry his head to our tree?
- Would we still be best friends?
- And if he died after 60 years of me dragging his head around, would I still attend our meetings with his taxidermized head and speak and chew chaw for both of us until Nazis cut down the Phil-and-Phil tree for firewood to help them burn effigies of love and sanity, forcing me to carve "Phil-and-Phil" into the flesh over my heart and bleed out our names until I was no more?

Truthfully or not, I answered all the questions correctly in Phil's opinion, and while I avoided confrontations thusly, he cut our names even deeper, which he could do now without looking, without breaking eye contact with me.

Therefore, I needed a break.

Therefore, I skipped a hangout.

Our hangouts weren't planned, not really. It was just assumed we would hang out every day until death. Well, I skipped one.

And I braced myself for something bad to happen.

Why?

Maybe it was Phil's knife work, or his relentless interest in my devotion to the cause, which was us. In addition, gut reasons.

"Of all the people we know," I said to my Gut, "who's the most likely to stab us to death with his knife?"

My Gut didn't answer. He'd already told me hundreds of times.

I pictured Phil sitting alone under the lean-to, waiting for me to show up, carving my name so much deeper, wondering what's keeping me.

He checks the sky—no blizzard—then the ground. No flood. No Nazis.

*What could it be?*

He rises, knife in hand, and walks a straight line to my house, a line taking him through woods, gardens, graveyards, into strangers' houses, over couches, over families, and out windows, then he knocks on my door with the point of the knife…

I waited, I wondered.

But nothing happened.

I went back to our tree the next day. Phil said nothing about my absence. We just started talking and trying to have fun again.

Clearly, Phil was reasonable. My nonappearance hadn't fazed him. So, I decided to skip a lot more. Instead of hanging out every day of the week, I pushed it back to three times a week, then two, then one.

That's when Phil called my house.

"It's for you," said Mom.

I put the phone to my ear—"Hello?"—then I heard what sounded like a whispery, faraway voice rising up out of some haunted well.

"Wanna hang out?" said Phil.

"Oh darn," I said. "I can't today."

And that's when he surprised me by asking, "Why?"

Since I hadn't anticipated being questioned, though I should have, I didn't have an answer, not a good one anyway: "Yeah, sorry. I just... I can't?"

"Why?"

"Because."

After a long silence from him, if you don't count homicidal mouth breathing, he said it again: "Why?"

"Well... because..."

"*Why?*"

I began to panic. How many whys did this kid have? How many times could I say "because" before he struck truth:

Dan is done with Club Phil-and-Phil.

And what would he do when he found out?

This question made me so nervous that instead of saying "because" again, I folded:

"Actually, you know what? I think I *can* hang out now."

I braced myself for another "why?" A "why?" that would take us right back to "because" territory, but he didn't say it, thank goodness. He said, "Good. See ya at the fort."

"See ya."

After that day, I scrapped my "because" and used something way better. I used lying. I couldn't believe I hadn't thought of it before.

"Oh, rats. Sorry, I can't."

"Why?"

"I have chores, homework, a recent grounding, and grandparents who drop by randomly. They're here! They're sick! Now I am sick. It's flu. Flu season is in my body to stay, and I've got grandparents and other relatives in distant hospitals. Gotta visit daily, and shucks, I'll likely get sicker there and be out of commission for months, if I even live, and even if I *do* live, I've got all these doggone and randomly scheduled funerals now. Sorry!"

I trimmed our hangouts down to once a month, but into those hangouts, Phil packed a month's worth of staring, interrogation, and knifework.

The tree looked unwell.

It was dropping leaves and drying up. It was quickly spending its life through the wound of our friendship.

*If something doesn't stop this friendship soon*, I thought, *the tree will die, and if there is a God, it'll fall on Phil.*

So, the friendship had to end.

For both our sakes.

*

And, the friendship did end.

It came crashing down in two scary events.

## Scary Event One, In Which I Get Another Call From Phil And Then A Call That Really Surprises Me

I got another call from Phil and explained I had chores and the flu and was later being dragged to a family reunion at a funeral parlor.

Not long after we hung up, however, I got another call, the really surprising one, a call from Phil's older brother:

James, the one and only.

Why was he calling *me*?

Why me and not Joe?

Because my brother had gotten himself a girlfriend. This meant that, more and more, James had no one to hang out with. He started calling me, and what a wonderful blessing.

It's a miracle for a child when he acquires anything that once belonged to his older brother.

Especially if it's a friend.

Friendship with James was fantastic not only because it had once belonged to Joe, but because James was an adventurer like me. Together, we biked, hiked, climbed trees, broke into cabins, vandalized middle-school playground equipment at night, and together we had no time for lean-tos, tree carving, or interrogations.

But back to that first phone call.

James wanted to hang out, so spank the Devil daily and the dirty gods be praised!

"Excuse me?" he said.

"Sorry, that's just what I say when I'm happy. Of course I want to hang out."

But there were dangers. I explained them: I'd already said no to Phil, which meant I was sick and doing chores at funerals.

James didn't care. He said we could meet secretly on the road. If Phil looked for us at their house or mine, he wouldn't find us.

Unfortunately, we were young and dumb: The road we picked to meet on secretly was the road right in front of James's house. That's where I was to meet him, right out front, in full view, easily visible for anyone who happened to be living in that house at the time.

To James's credit, he slipped out the front door silently and took up his bike even more silently, then off we went.

However, when we were thirty feet away, or way less, we heard it…

Behind us, somewhere in the extremely near distance:

- a heavy front door slammed
- little footsteps thumped speedily across a porch
- a voice shouted at our backs: "Wait!"

It was Phil.

"Where are you *going!*" This was Phil too.

He was furious. "I thought you had funerals! I thought you had flus!"

He was *very* furious.

James looked at me and whispered, "Go. *Go!*"

Now Phil hollered, "Stop! STOP!"

We did *not* stop.

"Where are you GOING?!" Each word cranked his voice up to a higher power of hate and volume, from a holler to a yell to a roar to a scream.

We didn't answer. We continued pedaling desperately down the road.

Phil screamed again: "Answer me!"

This command sounded so grown up, so villainous and dramatic, that James and I made the mistake of laughing.

Phil cracked.

He started jumping up and down and throwing things over the porch railing, anything he could get his hands on and lift, everything—rocking chairs, shoes, his bike, his mother's flowers—and for every item he threw, he screamed, "I *HATE* YOU!"

We pedaled as fast as we could while Phil screamed his hatred in a new way, drawing out each word: "I Haaaaaaate YOOOOOOOOOOOU!"

I wanted to drown out the eerie tension with more laughter, but when I glanced at James, I could tell by his gritted teeth and wide eyes that he was afraid.

He had the look of someone who'd done more than upset a little brother.

He looked like someone who knew there would be consequences.

Big ones.

*Bad* ones.

As I hurried away from Phil's screams, I wondered what he'd be capable of if someone pushed him even further.

If someone pushed him way too far...

## Scary Event Two, In Which We Pushed Phil Even Further, All The Way To Way Too Far

One day, James biked to my house. When he showed up, I said the usual: "Does Phil know?"

"No," said James.

Good enough for me.

But it shouldn't have been.

I should have said, "Are you *sure?*" a dozen times, but I didn't because, as I said before,

young and dumb.

James and I built bike ramps on the lawn. We had all the tools we needed:

- plywood
- cinderblocks
- two-by-fours
- and a hatchet for altering the two-by-fours and plywood to make different genres of jump.

We raced toward the ramps and flew. We landed, crashed, and laughed then flew again.

And I knew:

This is friendship.

Sure, there were hardships surrounding this new alliance—James's cooling connection with Joe, my freezing-over connection with Phil—but these were hard things for other people, not me. I didn't feel their sting. I didn't feel a thing.

While hanging out with James, I felt only speed, wind, air, and joy.

An hour into our fun, I happened to look up the road in front of my house, and I saw a small figure.

It was walking down the road.

Walking our way.

The figure was small because of the distance. But it was also small because it was small.

A child.

A little child about the size of...

### Phil.

Deep in the country, little children don't often walk down the road like this. They ride their bikes.

If they're out walking, they either just escaped from a neighbor's basement, or they're on their way to harm someone, maybe an old friend.

I whispered, "James."

He looked where I was looking and whispered, "Shit."

We stood there, side by side, watching Phil as he walked and walked. Something about his small size made it seem like he would never reach us, which made his increasing nearness surprising, almost unnatural, as if he was taking backwards steps on a forward moving walkway that was bringing him closer and closer. Slowly.

*And so quickly.*

Mesmerized by this optical illusion, James and I could do nothing but stand still and watch.

Of course we watched. It's what kids do. They lock their eyes on the most interesting thing, even if that thing is frightening.

Especially if it is.

At last, Phil somehow reached the edge of the lawn.

There, he stopped.

There he stood, staring at us. He didn't move. We didn't move.

I whispered, "What's he doing?"

"Whatever it is," whispered James, "it's *bad*."

Phil still didn't move. We still didn't either.

Suddenly, a car appeared on the road. I hoped it was Phil's parents here to take him to an asylum. But the car only slowed down a little, slow enough to get a good look at what must have appeared to be a low-stakes showdown in Kid Town.

The car passed on.

But something about its passing severed the leash keeping Phil in place—God's leash or the Devil's—and he went from complete stillness to sudden running, running at us in a straight line, as straight as a flatline, and *fast*, all in the blink of an eye.

James and I were transfixed. We stared at Phil's expressionless and intriguing face. How can a face look so calm while its body is knifing through the air at you with the savagery of a broken-free plane propeller?

As Phil neared, James spoke to him gently: "Okay, Phil. Take it easy, Phil. *Phil?*" But it wasn't okay, not for Phil, and he was *way* past taking it easy.

He couldn't slow down.

He could only go faster.

Without discussion, James and I started backing up.

But when Phil was six hundred and sixty-six centimeters from us, he stopped again. He stopped as suddenly as he had started, and he stood there breathing heavily through his nostrils' flarings like a tiny, lethal bull.

After an eternal second, Phil spoke:

"Hi, guys. What are you guys up to? You look like you're right in the middle of having a lot of fun. *Are* you? Are you right in the middle of having a lot of fun?"

It sounded friendly if you didn't pay attention to the tone or menacing repetition or who it was coming from.

I was about to answer when Phil's eyes dropped to the ground.

Not the ground, actually.

His eyes dropped to the hatchet lying on the ground ten feet from the toes of his sneakers.

Long before I knew what was happening, both Phil and James were in motion.

Apparently, James had seen something I hadn't, something in the eyes of his little brother, something murderous, and the realization that Phil was going to do something outrageous came to James and Phil simultaneously, which is why, in that instant, Phil launched and James leaped.

Their aim?

The hatchet, of course, so the Devil's bottom glowed with spank-joy and the dirty gods hid their faces.

In other words, Phil got to the hatchet first.

But just as his hands wrapped around the handle, James's foot came down on the hatchet, pinning Phil's fingers to the ground. What followed was a scream of frustration and fury, a ghostly scream, the scream of a ghost who has transformed his stolen well into a heavenward bullhorn of hate.

Phil thrashed, shrieked, and wailed, and James leaned onto his pinning foot like someone snuffing out a very nasty and powerful younger insect.

The brothers were spellbinding, a living statue of Cain and Abel, and I got to watch.

I watched without compassion. I had no room for it. I was full to the top with fear and wonder.

Eventually, Phil slipped his fingers free. He fell back onto the lawn and lay there or laid there, it's impossible to say which. He stared at the sky as if awaiting new orders from whatever power of the air had sent him that day.

Then he blinked.

Then he stood.

Next, he turned around and walked calmly back across the lawn, to the road again, then away.

And that was the end of Phil-and-Phil.

We never hung out again.

James and I got back to jumping our bikes. Or we tried to. Something about the fear of death, which makes bike jumping fun, wasn't fun anymore that day.

It felt better to be grounded.

Better to be alive and not mess with it.

I walked the hatchet back to the garage, feeling the blade with my thumb, and knowing how easily it could spell my name right through my ribs.

All the way down to my heart.

*

Whenever I saw Phil after that scary afternoon, I saw a blankness on his face when he aimed it my way, the kind of blankness you see on gravestones.

They keep their secrets.

What the stones do say isn't much: Just a couple of deeply carved names.

Names that seem to mean less and less in time.

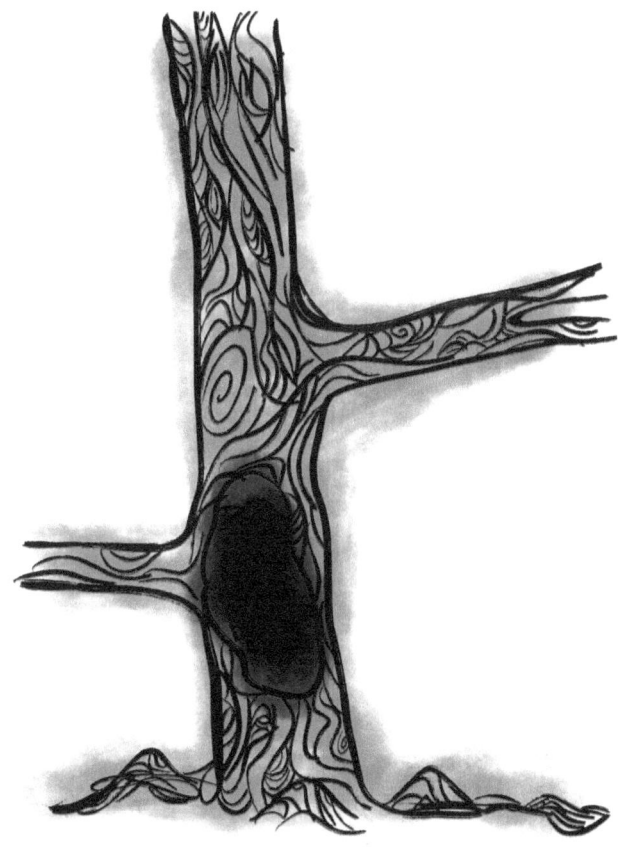

your doodles, memories, illustrations, story ideas...

**LESSON 26:**

# To Discover How Much a Girl Really Likes You, Ruin Your Life Right in Front of Her

The Walters family arrived at our little, country church and shocked us all by being people we'd never seen before. It was almost a bylaw that we had no new people in our pews. Unless they were babies. But a baby is just a copy of old things, which is what allowed the babies to slip into our congregation and act as if they belonged.

The Walters also shocked us by the gorgeousness of their daughter, Amy, who instantly troubled all the romantic plans of the young. Couples soured, divided, and the broken pieces formed a covetous ring around her like communist satellites.

I was one of those satellites, the most faithful, gravitating so close I burned alive daily. Unfortunately, I was too young to catch Amy's eye. And, unfortunately again, I was and remain morbidly hopeful. There's so much romantical fluid in my eyes, when I look into the future, there's an oasis in every direction. Therefore, my epitaph will read, "My life was a beautiful curse."

Not long after the Walters showed up, Amy showed up at church with a lovely new best friend.

Sometimes the beautiful surround themselves with a collection of people who aren't beautiful. These are settings for the gem. This way, the hot person's self-esteem isn't threatened, and the non-hot folk get to have a powerful, hot person for a friend and defender. It's a sexy feudal system, and it isn't going anywhere.

But sometimes, when a hot person has somehow based their worth on more than hotness, they can afford to have hot friends.

This was the case with Amy. The friend?

Charlotte.

Very soon, whenever you saw Amy, you saw Charlotte too, and your heart divided. Unless your heart didn't need to divide because it chose them both. Which my heart did. Now,

I had a new orbit. It sent me around Amy, around Charlotte, then back to Amy. If you described my path with a love-red pen, you would be drawing infinity, and that was the measure of my desire and patience.

When pursuing ladies out of my league, which was the only kind of lady I ever pursued, I took the frog-in-boiling-water approach. They were the dazzling frog. I was the innocent water. "Hop in, friend. I am room-temperature. You'll hardly notice I'm *everywhere*. No danger whatsoever of falling in love with *me*." My allies? The force of time, proximity, and the heat of my passion. Slowly, over years, I would turn up the passion heat, until one day, the metaphor had no choice but to end. Otherwise, my old loves would all be dead and taste like chicken.

My patience and nearness earned me an invitation to the Walters' camp on Saint George's Lake. There, in the romantic grip of the woods and waters, I'd do what I did best: love the lords my goddesses with all my heart, soul, mind, and strength, and turn up that heat, degree by degree.

## The Lake Time

I would get to be with the Walters for an afternoon and evening of swimming, a sleepover, and then another love-drunk day of excruciating fun. Amy would be there, of course, and of course, Charlotte.

I recall that each member of the Walters family had a name of their own, but those names were faint and faraway to me while my beloveds were close. Still, I had to interact with these others: "Hey, kid, the one swimming next to Amy, let's have a swimming race," and, "You there, kid who has a blue bathing suit like Charlotte does, climb on the dock so I can shove you off."

We swam: diving, racing, having breath-holding competitions. We played King of the Dock, and though I thought of Amy and Charlotte as women, they were young enough to play King of the Dock too.

In other words, *physical contact.*

I threw lesser Walters left and right, always battling for a chance to battle my Amy, my Charlotte.

*I got to.*

I grabbed their wrists. They grabbed mine. I shoved them, they shoved me. Once, Amy tackled me into the water, and we fell on top of Charlotte. For a moment, all three of us were touching, tangled, lost in the underwater world, where sounds resemble the chugging of a giant heart beating with need. We disentangled ourselves and swam to the surface. I felt pre-marital and so lucky. Immediately, I added our pileup to the list of physical and verbal interactions I was busy deciphering in the back of my mind always, gauging the worth and meaning of every touch, word, glance, laugh, answer, question, cough, sigh, and silence. For example, when I was tottering on the dock's edge and Charlotte kicked me in the lower back, was that almost my butt? If so, are butts on the table for us now? And Amy's been tackling everyone, but is this just to camouflage the fact that she really only wants to tackle me, no one else, and to join lips with me firmly mid-tackle?

The swimming and games and the blissful agony of the swimming and games went on and on until Mr. and Mrs. Walters screamed, "Suppertime!"

We happily swam for shore and supper, but on the way, I felt a pain in my stomach. Something inside gave me a sinister pinch. A warm and low gurgle followed. Immediately, it became dangerous to scissor my legs as freely and powerfully as usual.

I knew this feeling.

I called it the "cheese feeling," though it took me years to realize how accurate the name was. Back then, I called it the cheese feeling because it sounded funny, and because of phrases like, "who cut the cheese?" and "*I* cut the cheese." Somehow, I never connected the feeling to literal cheese. All I knew was this: The feeling led to some serious toilet time.

Nowadays, because my animalistic child-mind has become thoughtful and scientific, I can connect my cheese feeling that day to the meal I'd eaten before the Walters picked me up: a massive lunch of grilled cheese, yogurt, cheese squares, cheese sticks, cheese balls, Cheetos, a pint of milk, and I chased it all with ice cream stolen from the freezer when Mom wasn't looking because she was turning the dining room into a snow globe of grated parmesan.

That's what my intolerant gut was cooking with.

After all the swimmers got to shore for supper, the Walters honored me by serving my favorite food: endless pizza.

I ate the way every adventurous, lovesick child eats when on display before his crushes. I turned it into a competition. Everyone except the parents fought for the title, even Amy and Charlotte, and they tied for second place. Six slices apiece.

But I won.

*Nine.*

For an hour after supper, while digesting, we made fires, hunted leeches, and threw rocks at ducks. When the hour ended, we ran back to the water.

The cheese feeling was gone. Mostly. It came back once or twice, and I had to be very still, which sometimes got me shoved from the dock, and sometimes made me sink down into the dark and chilly lake to wait it out.

A mighty, muscle-locked ball of a boy, full of brewing consequences.

Many busy hours later, hours of me getting closer to love one iota's width at a time, it was time for bed. I went to bed, sighed many sighs, rested my back from the weight of the long, long game, then I fell asleep.

In the middle of the night, I woke.

In the middle of the night, I woke with a problem: I was going to explode in three seconds.

**One second**: I slipped from bed without a sound.

**Two seconds**: I followed the nightlight trail to the bathroom, shoved aside the bathroom door, which was nothing but a brown sheet of thin cloth.

**Two-point-five seconds**: I turned on the bathroom light. There was no bathroom fan. *God, no. NO FAN?!* There never had been. Never would be.

**Three seconds**: I sat.

**Three-point-one seconds**: I exploded.

If you've never spent the night in a lakeside cabin in the woods in Maine, you should know there's nowhere on Earth quieter than that. You can hear a sneeze on the other side of the lake, half a mile away. You can hear the blood flow of a hunting spider. You can hear the music playing in somebody else's dream.

And you can hear atomic diarrhea very well when it's 10 feet away, at most, from everyone in your cabin.

I tried hard to be quiet. I failed. My attempts were like trying to silence a shotgun with a rotten cabbage.

Finally, the nightmare stopped. I sat there as quiet as could be, sweating, my heart pounding, and I listened for any sign that any member of the Walters family was awake and aware.

I heard nothing.

Correction, I heard a sneeze from across the lake. I heard the pumping cold blood of the spider hanging over my head, a poor spider plugging its noses. But when it came to the music of the dreamers' dreams, I heard nothing. Maybe the Walters were a people who didn't dream. Maybe they were a people who slept so soundly they made you feel like you were thankfully alone in the cabin where you'd just done something devastating.

I listened and listened and didn't hear a single snort or snore. Not one twang of a bed spring. No adorable nighttime toots from the buttocks of the admired. This was the silence of a tomb in a cave near a lake in the deep, dark woods of Maine.

I thanked God for the fact that the family was asleep, so dead asleep that someone could have blasted a murky cabbage from the end of a twelve gauge that night and no one would have stirred.

I went back to bed. I slept the sleep of the relieved.

I woke.

Somehow, it was still the middle of the night. And, once again, I had only three seconds to react.

**One second**: Out of bed. No sound.

**Two seconds**: I lunged through the bathroom door, that semi-sheer sheet.

**Two point five seconds**: Bathroom light. No fan whatsoever. Never. Of course not. Who needs one of those desperately anyway?

**Three seconds**: Explosion.

**Aftermath**: Sweat. My thundering heart. I listened for signs of wakefulness.

Zero signs. The silence of a dead world, praise God.

Back to bed.

It happened three more times, possibly seven, over and over until I'd finally exorcised the last of the cheese feeling and was able to sleep. I slept long and hard. So long and hard, it was 10 AM by the time I woke up and realized the sun was in the wrong place. A scary place. *Super late.*

I heard sounds of splashing.

Everyone was up already, *for hours*, up and full of breakfast, and through the necessary digestion hour—burning things, killing leeches, and duck hunting without me—and then out onto the dock for war.

And they'd let me sleep.

Why? I wondered.

Maybe they were the kind of family that didn't wake sleeping guests. This made sense. They couldn't know the morning rules of non-relatives. For all they knew, waking me was dangerous. I might die or attack. And if this was true about them, maybe Charlotte, also a guest, was still in bed like me. Maybe I would leave my bedroom and bump into her on her way to the bathroom and race ahead of her to make sure it was okay in there, and then come out, wait for her, and we'd have a thrilling chat in the hallway and then step out of the cabin a bonded pair.

But Charlotte wasn't in the cabin.

I was the only one.

I peeked into the bathroom to see if I'd done a good coverup. I smiled. I'd done a *very* good coverup. But I stopped smiling when I realized I'd done such a good coverup that it couldn't possibly be mine. The toilet looked reborn, as if it had not only been triple flushed, but scrubbed with a toothbrush, maybe a wire brush, and then thrown away and replaced with a new toilet.

But who had done it? It couldn't have been Amy and Charlotte, working together in long, yellow gloves, laughing as they gagged and scrubbed. It couldn't, because that would mean there is no God.

It had to be the parents. Parents are the protectors of the family. They have no choice but to wake up for sounds that no one else can possibly hear. Yes, it was them, Mr. and Mrs. Walters. They'd swept in after me and made sure the toilet was pristine and a brand-new toilet for Amy and Charlotte, ensuring that they would suspect nothing.

Bless them.

But why had they done it? Had I left evidences? And if Mr. and Mrs. cleaned because of remaining evidences, did they know what these evidences pointed to, *who* they pointed to? If they didn't know, if they'd studied whatever had accidentally been left behind and learned nothing, maybe they'd asked around, confronting person after person while I slept, eliminating potential culprits until the truth was known by one and all.

Somehow, I didn't believe this to be true. I forced into existence the possibility that maybe there was nothing to worry about. A sparkling toilet? No big deal. It was merely the aftermath of a regularly scheduled, alarmingly vigorous toilet cleaning. An uncomfortable coincidence, nothing more.

I also allowed that it was possible the parents *did* know it was me, having smelled smells and heard sounds that had never come from a Walters before, but they'd kept it quiet. My secret was safe with them. Because they were good people, and there is a God.

When I stepped out of the cabin into the deep-morning sunshine, I stepped out cautiously, wondering and praying. Fearing. And of course, hoping.

*No one knows*, I thought, *please, God, no one knows. If they do, let it be the parents. And, Father, make them keep it to themselves. Force them.*

I stood at the bottom of the cabin steps, looking at the lake. There, all the youths were splashing around. Amy, the dock's one and only king, shoved people beautifully while Charlotte swam like an angel in skimpy blue. Everyone was laughing, battling, splashing, singing, all drunk on summer loveliness, and I could tell not one of them was thinking anything mortifying about one of their dear companions.

*They don't know*, I realized. *That's not what people look like when they know something horribly embarrassing about a beloved member of their inner circle. Thank you, God.*

But the longer I looked, the more I thought the swimmers and dock battlers seemed a little off: Even after a long night of perfectly uninterrupted sleep, they all appeared to be somewhat sluggish, drowsy, as if their sleep hadn't been so perfect and uninterrupted after all. But no, that wasn't it, I decided. Not even close. They were just worn out from the wildness of yesterday.

I took a long breath of late-morning air and let it out slowly. *The parents know*, I thought. *That's all. Amy and Charlotte don't know. They'll never know. Because the parents are good. They're good people. God, force them to be good people for the rest of their lives.* After my deep and satisfying breath, the only thing to do was to have some cold pizza for breakfast, put on my bathing suit, and go taste the waters with my loves.

Just as I was about to duck back inside to feed and change, I heard someone say, "Good morning there, champ."

I turned and saw the father approaching me. He walked slowly with his hands held behind his back. He looked exactly like a man with something to say that would make a bosom friend of the family extremely uncomfortable.

*Lord, please no.*

"Good morning, Mr. Walters," I said, trying to sound strong. I needed to sound exactly like a person in control of himself, someone whose body would never betray him all night long. *It wouldn't dare.*

"Good morning," he said, again.

Why did he say it again? Is it because the thing he has to say is so difficult to say he'd rather say good morning to me for the rest of our lives?

He stopped walking toward me but only because he was standing beside me. We looked at the water, the swimmers, the sky. It would have been nice if he'd said nothing, if he'd communicated everything by standing there silently. Because some things, if left unsaid, are survivable. Silence allows you to imagine a conversation that would be much easier to bear than the real thing. Imagine it: two men, talking without a word. Our quiet sounds so nice. It sounds like this:

> **WALTERS**: I vaguely overheard what happened last night, but my wife and I were the only ones who heard, believe me. We're *extremely* light sleepers. That's the only way we heard because it really wasn't that deafening at all. And we took care of the lavatory for you before anyone else woke up. Be at peace: The girls will never know.

**DAN**: You *are* good people. I have a feeling you're the type of people who will be good for a lifetime, and you'll probably even take some things with you to the grave.

**WALTERS**: Of course. That's one of our main reasons for going to the grave.

Two silent men. One sighs, the other sighs, but most importantly, everything is okay.

But it wasn't okay, because instead of communicating wordlessly, Mr. Walters said, "Rough night?"

I tried to answer, but my throat had contracted to a thread of ice.

"Feeling any better now, champ?"

I managed to say "yes" with enough wind and moisture in my throat to sound like a living, human boy.

"Good," he said with a chuckle. "I thought we were going to have to call the hospital for a minute there."

I took this heat as well as I could. I thanked him for his concern. The hospital? How thoughtful. An image passed through my mind: A boy on a toilet being airlifted (toilet and all) to the nearest medical facility. I would have laughed at this image, but I could barely breathe or summon the willpower to circulate my blood, so laughing was out.

I only survived the conversation because I still had hope: Yes, the parents knew, but no one else. How did I know? Again, because the parents were good, and I had proof of their goodness. They'd invited me to this camp. They'd given me pizza. They'd attacked my ground zero with soap and elbow grease until it gleamed. And they'd given birth to Amy, who was responsible for Charlotte. They *were* good people. People who would never tell.

Though Mr. Walters *had* called me "champ." Twice.

Suddenly, I doubted, and this opened the door for more doubt.

Of course they'd told. Parents have no choice. When someone in the house is getting murdered by diarrhea, they must know who. Otherwise, how can they help? Once again, I imagined the parents asking around, whispering so as not to wake me:

"Someone almost died on the toilet last night," said Dad to Amy. "Was it you?"

"No."

"What about you?" said Mom to Charlotte.

"No."

"How about the rest of you kids, was it you?"

Then I imagined something much, much worse. I pictured the parents' eyes opening at the same instant in the middle of the night. A sound had broken their slumber. There it was again. Close. *It's inside the cabin.* And then again, and again, and *again*. Until other eyes opened in the dark.

All the eyes.

Then I imagined so many laughing faces buried in pillows, so many people fighting hard to be silent in case anyone out there in the night was dying for some privacy.

There I stood with the father. We looked at the water and the sky. Believe it or not, I still had hope. True, my hope balanced on an ice cube melting in the same pot I used for boiling women, but I still had it.

We watched the swimmers. And that's when I saw the truth and lost my hope:

One swimmer happened to look our way, and then another and another. Soon, they were all looking our way, Amy and Charlotte included, stopping their games to look. The troubled waters flattened. Heads floated, Charlotte's head too, while Amy stood on the dock as tall as a goddess of secret knowledge.

They all stared at the astonishing boy, the boy who had done the impossible: With his body alone, he'd produced more than three times the weight of a boy in a single night. It was a miracle cut from the same cloth as the feeding of the five thousand, though Jesus's miracle earned an encore mine would never receive.

The swimmers went back to their play, a new game involving lots of whispers and laughing.

"Glad you're alive," said the father, chuckling again.

*I* wanted to be glad, but it was too soon. "Thank you," I said, and the father patted me on the shoulder then went into the cabin.

I stood alone.

Ahead of me, a long, long day of fun.

All I had to do now was have some cold pizza, put on my bathing suit, then somehow live for the rest of my life.

# LESSON 27:

# There is *Everything* to Be Afraid of in the Dark

To help me conquer my fear of the dark, Mom would say, "There's nothing in the dark that isn't in the light."

She also said, "When you're scared, read the Bible."

I did.

But that's how I bumped into this: "Thou makest darkness, and it is night: wherein all the beasts of the forest do creep forth."

This explained why our cats showed up every morning with blood on their hands. Because cats are beasts. So are wolves and bears. Suddenly the darkness was a vast puzzle, and every piece was a beast. Pieces that moved like gears. This interlocking system of teeth could easily grind up a small boy. Arguably, that's what the system's for.

I also found this in the Bible: "Men loved darkness rather than light, because their deeds were evil. For every one that doeth evil hateth the light, neither cometh to the light, lest his deeds should be reproved."

Whatever that meant. I asked what it meant. Mom said it meant bad people didn't want to get caught, that's all. This I understood. I hated getting caught too. But good brother Joe said it meant evil people love the dark because it's their camouflage. It helps them kidnap and kill little Bible-reading boys without ever being seen.

Like a parent's heart grows to make room for additional children, my fear of the dark grew to make room for this additional information.

"Try praying," said Mom.

I asked God, *Dear God, do innocent, Bible-loving boys ever get kidnapped and killed in the dark?*

No answer. In other words, "What do you think?"

\*

I once had a friend (Matthew the Brave) who fought his fear of the dark by facing it head on.

Often at night, while walking upstairs from a darkened downstairs, he'd get that awful

feeling. You know the one: Something's behind you, its long fingers spreading, stretching, reaching for your ankle. As soon as this feeling started coiling around Matthew's heart, throat, and ankle, he'd stop right where he was on the stairs and wait.

Without looking back, he'd breathe in.

Breathe out.

Then he'd do the unthinkable:

He'd step backwards, down to the previous step. Then down again, and again, sinking himself deeper and deeper into the awful feeling.

When he reached the darkened first floor, he'd stand there, unmoving, waiting until the feeling went away before he tried the stairs again. And the feeling always did go away, though sometimes it came back, and he'd have to do his backwards walk again, occasionally two or three times in a row.

My friend said I should try it.

"Why?" I asked.

"To stop being scared of stairs at night."

"But that's how I survive stairs at night. Without being scared, how would I know when I'm about to die and that I need to run? I think I'll keep my fear and survive, thanks."

And I have: I've run up the stairs every night for 40 years, and every night of the 40, I've lived.

\*

Another friend told me he'd killed his fear of the dark by not dying in the dark.

"Explain," I said.

"Logic," he said. "I've been in the dark half my life and nothing bad has happened yet. And every time I survive the dark again, the chances get higher that nothing bad ever *will* happen. By now, the chances of surviving are so good, my fear of the dark is just gone."

I saw his point. But all my friend had to do was die in the dark once to ruin his theory.

I tried to tell him this and added what the Bible says about evil people, how they love the dark because it helps them kidnap and kill, but he believed in his logic too much to believe me.

And though I don't hope he'll get kidnapped or killed one night, it sure would help my argument.

\*

Naturally, the people who have most often exploited my fear of the dark for fun have been family members. For they have almost unlimited access to me.

## One

When we visited Uncle Clarence, he used to torment me with a challenge: "You can have this dollar if you walk out back, cross the field, go all the way to the woods, and stand there for thirty seconds. Then shout as loud as you can, 'I am not afraid!' Wait another thirty seconds, then walk back. Don't run."

This was mean. I wanted that money, but I also wanted to live, and Clarence knew it. He knew his money was safe and sound, and visit after visit I stayed alive, poor, and bitter.

## Two

Sometimes in the evening while talking with Joe, his eyes would suddenly leap from my face to the dark window behind me. He'd point and scream, and I'd scream, and run from the window.

Our cat also did this to me. I'd be petting her masterfully, exactly the way she taught me to, then she'd look past my face to whatever dark window was closest and freeze, her eyes wide with horror and attraction. There was never anything there, but I'd fall for it every time. I'd turn to the window fast, get scratched, and while I stared at my terrified reflection, I'd get to see my face as Joe saw it: painted with hilarious terror. It was a perfect face to laugh at: supernova eyeballs over a blackhole mouth big enough to fit the cat. Who could blame Joe? Not me. I laughed too.

## Three

Joe and I were walking out to the barn one night. I would never have done this normally, but there was something out there calling to us: Joe's crow.

He'd found the large bird in the woods by following its yelling or swearing for help. With crows, there's no difference. Mr. Crow got hurt somehow and stranded way up on a branch. The stalagmite of droppings rising from the ground beneath its butt let us know the poor thing had been there for a long time. With bravery and care, Joe climbed the tree, bagged the bird, brought it home, and then nursed it back to health.

He named the crow Raven to help with its self-esteem and built a cage for it on the side of the barn. He fed Raven nitrate-loaded deli meat, enough to put the bird at the top of cancer's hit list, but we didn't know this then. It was the 80s, back when cancer was our favorite food.

Joe and I headed for Raven's cage with a handful of thinly sliced ham, and we were armed. A hatchet for Joe, a machete for me. We had a flashlight, but we didn't turn it on because the beam made Raven attack the cage.

Walking side by side, Joe and I pushed our way into the dark, getting farther and farther from the house. Soon, we were close enough to the barn to feel its enormous presence. It seemed to come out of nowhere. Scary how something that big can sneak up on you. I tried not to think of anything frightening, such as who or what might be hiding in the barn; or the story Dad told us about the crazy lady he knew who said over and over, "There's nothing in my closets. You won't find anything at all in *my* closets"; or the stories we'd heard about the farm where my grandmother lived when she was a little girl, the farm where something was living in the attic. It came down once or twice a year and stood beside the beds of the sleeping family, and sometimes it grabbed them by the hair and shook them so violently they had bruising on their scalps. I wasn't doing a very good job with my thinking, but I had my machete, Joe was right beside me, and we were almost at Raven's cage.

Just as we rounded the corner of the barn, we heard a horrible sound: the quick thudding of footsteps. Something running. Heading right for us. Almost as soon as we heard this, the running person or thing was close enough to strike, and that's when the world filled with a terrible light and a monstrous roaring.

Without hesitation, I flung the ham and dropped my machete. It fell through my fingers as if they were made of water. Then I fell on the ground too. *I* was water. Forgetting I'd fallen, I tried to run away, but all my legs could do was spin me in circles.

At this point, the monster, the running roarer, started laughing, which gave the monster away. It was Dad. He laughed and laughed and eventually I was able to stop going in circles, take his reaching hand, and let him help me to my feet.

I thought at first his laughter was all for me, and I was angry, but then I saw where he was shining his flashlight: at Joe, who gotten himself all the way to the far end of the lawn and was on the ground like I had been. Joe got up and headed toward us, picking up his ax on the way. The roar had made him throw his ax. Backwards. Away from our attacker.

As Joe jogged back, he was smiling like wolves do when they're actually sheep in wolves' clothing. I was smiling too.

Dad continued laughing and Joe and I laughed, grateful that we weren't murdered, and while Dad described to us what we'd looked like, we picked up pieces of thrown ham.

After feeding Raven, we went inside to tell Mom what had happened. Joe and I reenacted our terror, miming the flinging of meat, the dropping of machetes, and the throwing of axes, backwards. We cried out and fell to the floor, our legs running us in circles while Mom and Dad laughed.

And the puzzle of blood-thirsty bears, wolves, and killers looked in through the windows at the family's fun, admiring what they had made.

your doodles, memories, illustrations, story ideas...

## LESSON 28:

# You Can Ruin Biology With Your Chemistry

We thought we knew what school was.

It was homework, papers, the barbed and poison-dipped social ladder, the endless facts and figures sliding over our long-term memory without making a dent.

But then school changed. It gave us knives. It gave us jars full of the dead.

I remember the awful smell of the preservative liquid. I remember the vulgarity of a spreadeagled frog. I remember going outside the lines of the day's assignment to cut off the head of my fetal pig then wondering if this made me evil. But when I looked around and saw everyone else was decapitating too, I felt much better. "I'm not evil," I thought. "I'm a typical member of this society."

And I remember Tom and Matt.

Tom was a death metal guy. He wore all black all the time, rattled his 10-foot wallet chain like a Victorian ghost, and was known for sitting so still he looked dead, but then, out of nowhere, he'd have one of his legendary fits.

Witness a Tom fit:

We students are standing at our biology tables, peeling animals like bananas, and the teacher, Mr. Martin, is at the far end of the room, a safe distance.

One of us turns to Tom and whispers, "Do it, Tom." Someone else whispers, "Do it, Tom. Do it, Tom." Quickly, a chant develops.

Tom pretends not to hear but we know he hears because he's become as still as a demon locked in a coffin of ice.

But then, without warning, out of the grave of his stillness, he jumps up and down over and over while waggling his tongue, and though he puts one hand to his forehead and makes the sign of the Devil, the most Satanic thing about him is the height of his vertical leap. It's so impressive. Too impressive for someone who hates athletics as much as Tom. Clearly, he's getting help from the Devil to be so sporty.

Tom would do all this jumping, Satan signing, and waggling in the two seconds it took Mr. Martin to turn his head. By the time Martin had his eyes on Tom's corner of the room, Tom was back to cutting a dead animal's heart out like he was supposed to, looking as sedate as ever, not even breathing hard.

Then one day, after we said, "Do it, Tom! Do it, Tom!" Tom did something new.

He seized a pile of pig guts in a fist and danced his hell dance while the guts sent droplets of blood and chemicals flying and running down his veiny arm, splashing on the floor.

All in a blink.

When Mr. Martin looked over, it was over.

And we were changed.

From then on, when we said, "Do it, Tom," we meant "Grab guts, Tom! Grab guts and do it! DO IT, TOM!"

And he did. Again and again. With frogs, earthworms, mice, pigeons, fish, starfish, and rats, Satan giving him enough air that Tom could have slam dunked a hog's head to take the lead in the endless game of gore in hell.

Tom's wildness got to us. It took us places. It made a girl, Alison, start singing AC/DC lyrics louder and louder while she ripped skin and plucked guts. It made Tracy carve part of a Plath poem into a rabbit's ass.

And Tom's wildness made me point at a fish fin and say to Sam Baxter, "I'll give you a dollar—"

It was in his mouth before I could finish my sentence, the end being "if you eat that."

Tom's wildness also made Matt, a small, blond, massively popular kid, wait for Mr. Martin to look the other way. When Martin did, Matt hoisted a gallon jar that was full to the top with the preserved dead, and he threw it out the window.

The jar and its travelers soared and fell three stories to the field below. The jar broke. It exploded. Mr. Martin didn't hear it, and he hadn't seen. But *we* had seen. We'd watched Matt throw the jar and had gasped, and when we heard the semi-distant sound of glass shattering, Sam Baxter coughed out a starfish anus.

Mr. Martin turned around. Something had happened, but he didn't know what. His eyes searched the room but all he saw was good behavior: kids leaning over cats, rats, and rabbits and cutting their eyes out.

For the rest of class, we took turns sneaking glances out the window to enjoy the display of animals on the field below. And we took turns complimenting Matt and thanking him for his service.

Class ended. Somehow, there were no consequences. We walked toward the doorway on eggshells, waiting for Mr. Martin to stop us. He didn't. After we passed through door, no more eggshells: We hopped and skipped and praised our many gods.

Unfortunately, the next time we had class with Mr. Martin, he held up a big tray full of broken glass. The exploded dissection jar.

"Who did this?" he said.

No one moved. No one spoke.

"*Who* did this?" he said again.

We faced forward silently, good soldiers all, holding the line of loyalty.

We waited. What would happen next?

What happened next was Mr. Martin asked us, "Who did this?!" again and again, getting louder and louder until he shouted, "WHO **DID** THIS?!"

Still, we held our peace. Martin's eyes combed through us for the lice of guilt. His eyes touched on Sam. Sam swallowed a bat knuckle but said nothing. Martin glared at Alison who looked as innocent and scared as someone who'd never even heard of rock and roll or the heroin-level fun of publicly vandalizing school property. Next, Tracy. She went so pale she would have disappeared completely in a forest of Sylvia Plaths. Our Tracy, who would only ever harm the living, herself, never the dead. Mr. Martin's eyes shifted to me. I bore the weight as well as I could, trying to look like a puzzled, eager-to-please boy, a boy with snitch potential (If I only knew, sir, I'd tell you everything, I *swear* I would!). I also tried to look heartbroken and offended over what had happened to the animals, their jar, the special liquid. *What a waste*, said my face. *I wish so badly I had any information whatsoever so I could rat them all out immediately*, and it must have worked, because Martin looked from me to Tom. But Tom had been a freedom fighter since birth—birth had given him the idea. There was no shaking Tom; he would die with the truth locked up and suffocating behind his gnashing teeth.

Then it was Matt's turn.

The beams of Mr. Martin's vision struck Matt's eyes, and the sun stood still. The showdown. We held our breath. Didn't blink. We trembled. This staring match was so intense, it felt like Martin stared at all of us *through* Matt. We were a mushroom community connected in the underground, all rooted to the crime's creator.

Matt stared right back at Mr. Martin and demonstrated wonderful control: His face did not turn red. His eyes were dry. He didn't sweat or hiccup or jitter his way to a panic attack. And though he didn't look exactly innocent—through no fault of his own, it was the age—he carried no obvious signs of guilt.

Matt had won.

How did we know? Because Mr. Martin's eyes moved on. On and on until we'd all had our turn, and yet, no one broke.

This sent Mr. Martin into strategy mode. "Very well," he said, which sounded scary, and it was: "No more dissections until you tell me who did it."

Amazing.

How did he know exactly how to hurt us?

We'd expected him to use the usual threats—mass detention or suspension—but we never imagined he'd come up with something effective.

For the rest of the day, the rest of the week, biology class changed. No more decapitations. No more juggling eyeballs or making hand puppets out of Guinea Pig pelts. No more braceleting or ringing guts around our wrists and fingers. No more organ-squeezing leaps from Tom. What was left? Nothing. Absolutely only barebones, unincentivized, utterly forgettable education.

Mr. Martin lectured. On and on he talked in his dusty, droning, voice, sucking the romance right out of biology. While he talked, an interesting thing happened. Every brain in every head began to glare at Matt, our hero, and the small, popular boy grew smaller and smaller under the weight of our need to dissect again.

Dissection had brought out the best in us, the best in school. Our focus had been marvelous. Our work ethic? Perfect. English and math should have paid attention and found a way to incorporate corpses and knives. We would have been geniuses. But now we were nothing. Victims of the lecture. Stones weathering away in the eternal river of Mr. Martin's talk.

I don't know if somebody said something to Matt over the weekend or if he made his decision on his own. I only know that on Monday, he interrupted the lecture by standing up.

"Mr. Martin?" he said.

Martin stopped and looked at Matt. "Yes?"

We looked at Matt, waiting. He seemed smaller than ever, impossibly young and brave.

"I did it," Matt said. "I threw it out the window."

Mr. Martin took a deep breath using only his nose, like a bull would do. "And?"

"I'm sorry."

"*Why* did you do it?"

This caught Matt off guard. He'd expected punishment, but he hadn't expected to explain himself. And how could he explain? It was a very complicated thing. Yes, he threw the jar, but he was only a small portion of the power that made him do it. He was the hand, but the rest of the body was made of us, all of us. The mushrooms. All connected, making the entire class a single, wild beast. Matt was merely the part of the body that did the wildest thing. If it hadn't been him, it could have been any of us. Eventually, it would have been. So, it was *all* of us. Everyone threw that jar.

And yet, Matt stood alone.

"*Why?*" said Mr. Martin. "Why did you do it?"

"I don't know," Matt said, the first line of defense in childhood. But this was unacceptable.

"This is unacceptable," said Mr. Martin.

We ached as we watched Matt think. Because we had no idea what he would say, and especially because we had no idea what *we* would say. When the spirit of bad behavior leaves you, it's very difficult to remember why you just swallowed a fish fin or saluted Satan or made the sky rain rats and cats and frogs.

Then Matt answered:

"I did it... for a laugh, I guess?"

Mr. Martin frowned. "Who put you up to it?"

"No one," said Matt.

This was a lie. We all put him up to it, as I said. The dead animals too, and the knives. Mr. Martin as well, in a way. It was the system. But nobody's allowed to blame the system.

"So, you just decided to destroy school property... for a laugh?"

"Yes." And for the immortality of glory.

Martin frowned again, for obvious reasons, but maybe he also frowned because Matt's answer was too believable to be taken apart. It sounded like the truth, and the truth cannot be reduced to smaller, truer pieces. It's already the smallest piece, and the biggest. Put simply, the interrogation was done.

"Well," said Mr. Martin, looking disgusted, looking weary, "that's a detention."

"Thank you," said Matt, and he said it brilliantly, with enough sincerity in his voice to satisfy Mr. Martin (thank you for not suspending me), and enough hidden sass to satisfy us (screw you, The Man).

I don't know why Martin didn't give Matt a heavier punishment, but maybe I do. While the man glared at the small, courageous child, he sensed the larger body the boy was connected to. He sensed the one who was truly guilty: the entire body. If he could have, he would have suspended it, but how do you suspend a body when you can't prove there is a body, because it's metaphorical? What do you do?

You slap the wrist.

But maybe Mr. Martin was merciful for another reason too. Maybe he remembered what it felt like to be so young that your identity is putty, an adaptable puzzle piece that morphs to fit the needs of the larger puzzle, morphs to contribute and gain praise, but most importantly, to belong. Maybe he remembered that moving separately from the body you're connected to, ignoring its wants, needs, and commands, amputates you, isolates you, and this, for one so young, is death.

After Matt received his sentencing and sat, we waited for Martin's next move.

There was still an hour left of class. Plenty of time for dissection. And hadn't he promised we could have our knives back if the guilty came forward?

Mr. Martin shook his head. Mr. Martin sighed bitterly. Though a hand would be punished, the body had gotten away. But the body was children, and the body really had done a good job for weeks, leaving no organ uncarved, finding every last secret of anatomy, going about science as if it mattered.

Wearily, he pointed at the dissection cabinet where the dead rested, where the knives waited, and said, "Get to work."

We stood as one.

We rushed as one.

We, a single organism, got to work, our many pieces bound together by the magic of biology.

your doodles, memories, illustrations, story ideas...

## LESSON 29:

# It's So Easy to Lose Friends, There Shouldn't Be Any Friends Left

I had a bad best friend in 4th grade. He was bad in three ways.
Let's meet Timmy Varney.

## Bad Way One

Tim was better looking than me.

This wasn't his fault. He didn't select his shapes. However, Tim *did* lean into his good looks, having hygiene awareness, for example, and every time he went out in public, he was excessively easy to see and did nothing to douse his visibility.

He was *so* easy to see, in fact, if I was standing next to him, I was *not* seen.

For a middle child, being not seen is living death. When our spotlight flutters, winks out, or is blocked by cooler, more hygienic shapes, we die.

We zombify.

We groan, rot, and shuffle along, wishing we could take the advice of our fathers: "Dan, if something bothers you, beat it up or don't think about it."

"But I can't beat up Tim, he's my best friend."

"Okay. Well, when I had a problem, I always just played more sports. Try that."

"Will sports games make Tim ugly and smell like the rest of us? If so, I'll play *all* the sports games."

"It's 'sports.'"

"What?"

"It's not 'sports games,' it's just '*sports*,' but never mind; your younger sister and older brother are here. Let's stop talking and enjoy them."

## Bad Way Two

I did not own the greatest treasures of our age. *Tim* owned the greatest treasures of our age:

Ninja Turtles, G.I. Joes, Ghostbusters, Transformers, Crash Test Dummies, He-Mans, and the mighty Speak & Spell, a robot-voice toy bristling with 26 push buttons—the entire alphabet—which was excessive when all you needed the robot to say was "F U... F U... F U..." forever.

Clearly, the love language of Tim's parents was toys.

My native tongue.

When I went over to Tim's house and we played with his toys, love was no longer an abstract concept designed to be understood and felt only by younger and older siblings.

Nay, love was something I could hold in my hands (later, I would sniff my hands, for the perfume of rubber and plastic does linger). Love was something with articulating joints, nicknames like "Sergeant Slaughter," and often it was an ooze-green tank thing with a little ozone-smelling motor that hummed loudly, shot pizza pies, and bore a warning label telling you exactly what you were about to shoot your pizzas at:

"DO NOT SHOOT AT PEOPLE OR ANIMALS."

Tim's toys were so fun he could have been fifty times cleaner and better looking and I still would have play-dated him till death did us part.

## Bad Way Three

One day, Tim did a horrible, unthinkable thing...

I went over to his house. These visits had become increasingly medicinal for me: When away from his house and treasures, I had paranoia, irritability, sweats, and the shakes.

But being there?

It fixed me.

However, when we went to his room this time, I looked all around for my love fix and didn't see a scrap of it anywhere.

His many marvelous toys, which had formerly been everywhere, were nowhere to be seen.

"Where are all my many marvelous reasons for being here?" I said, though I used a friendly accent, which made it sound like this:

"Where are your toys?"

"Got rid of 'em," he said.

"What?"

"I got rid of my toys."

"I heard what you said. It's just, I don't understand what you said, and I never will. Again, *what*?"

"It was just time to grow up, ya know?"

I did *not* know. I was too stunned to know anything at all. I stood there, disoriented, nauseous, and praying for hallucinations. Even a sighting of love that wasn't there would have been better than what I was seeing.

Nothing.

It was so easy to see nothing, in fact, that's all I saw.

Horrible, unthinkable Tim was not seen.

Not one bit.

I would later cry, "I wish I'd asked him so many more questions!" But I'd been far too stunned for so many more questions. So, I've been asking them in daydream and nightmare encounters with Tim ever since:

- Yeah, but *how* did you get rid of them? Like are they maybe in a dumpster somewhere within walking distance?
- Did you give them to some local relative who's looking for a new best friend?
- Did you give them to charity?
- And what charity exactly?
- And maybe there's still time to get them back (the poor will always be with us, am I right?)
- And the greatest question of all, the one I wish I'd asked long before that awful day, the day love died:

"If you're ever in a mood for something effing insane like, I don't know, getting rid of your beautiful toys, would you pretend I'm a dumpster or a needy cousin or widows and orphans and let your growing-up problem be solved that way? You'll be free to grow up as much as you want. Sky's the limit! Just give me your toys, you inconsiderate bastard!"

But like I said, I was much too stunned. So stunned I wasn't much fun on that play date. I was all anxiety, fatigue, confusion, muscle aches, dilated pupils, and hunting all over Tim's house for my medicine.

In vain.

Therefore, I went home early.

I made up some excuse: "I think I have to go home to scream for thirty years."

Tim made up some excuse too: "Yes, please go home. We're not friends."

Picture a boy walking the long way home, a way taking him past every dumpster in the county.

This is the same boy who lived thirty years since that awful day, thirty long years, and yet he didn't realize something pretty incredibly obvious until writing this story:

- What if Tim only *said* he got rid of his toys?
- A *lie?!*
- Of course a lie.
- What if he lied because he figured out that I would be best friends with *anyone*, even Vlad the Impaler if Vlad happened to have twenty or more Ninja Turtle figures; fifty G.I. Joes (including Snake Eyes, "the silent assassin"); the Ghostbusters' Ectomobile; *every* Transformer; almost too many Crash Test Dummies; all the Masters of the Universe; and enough "F-U"s to lullaby a billion boys to sweet dreams of love?
- Oh yes, I would drink the blood of Christian babies for this love.
- I would even tolerate someone as extravagantly visible and me-eclipsing as Tim.

Now *that's* a bad best friend.

That's a friend you turn your back on, God be with you.

And may the Lord make His face shine upon you, Tim, casting the longest shadow at your back, a shadow in which a forty-three-year-old child shuffles rottily along, lost on the long way home, still anxious, sweaty, crabby, and confused.

Still looking, listening, and sniffing everywhere for love.

your doodles, memories, illustrations, story ideas...

**LESSON 30 (IN 10 PARTS):**

# There's More Than Sound and Fury in a Homemade Bomb: Sometimes, There's Love. In Other Words, the End of War

## Ten

The excitement of lighting a bomb is the excitement of lighting a birthday cake when you know for a fact that your craziest wish is going to come true in seven to ten seconds.

As a child, I knew this excitement well.

I lived for it.

That day, the day of the great bomb, I was in my room imitating people from church and recording myself on a tape player. Suddenly, Joe burst in. He was breathing heavily, his face red from running, and he was giggling, a sound that precedes many adventures.

"I need your help," he said.

I hadn't been needed by Joe for many days, so I was happy. Overjoyed even. Otherwise, I might have been clearheaded enough to use his need of me to make him suffer.

I could have ordered him to explain what he needed in detail and then tortured him with Mom's "I'll think about it," a phrase meaning she'd already thought about it with frightening speed and the answer was always no.

I could have said, "Dearest Joe, come back later. I'm busy," or "I'll help you if you let me look at your X-Men comics, play with your LEGOs, borrow your *Jurassic Park* trading cards, or if you can go one day without calling me stupid. Also, I want money."

Unfortunately, my overjoy got the better of me, and I quickly shouted "sure!" to whatever.

Without another word, Joe turned and ran, which meant I was to follow.

I did.

While following, I wondered why he needed me. Which skill of mine did he require? Did he need my speed? I was the fastest boy in my grade. Did he need my unique arm? I was the rock-skipping champion. Did he need my knives? I owned twenty times more knives than I had hands, and I knew how to wear them all on a single belt without injury.

Or maybe, just maybe—*please, let it be this*—he needed me to help him with the greatest thing of all:

## Bomb Work

I would have asked Joe my questions while following him down the hall, down the stairs, and out the front door, but I couldn't. We were running too fast, and he was giggling too hard, to speak.

We raced in single file along a grassy path, which bordered the family woods. It led to a deadly road, Route 3, a road as fast as a highway. It ripped through our little country town, killing pets and scaring parents like our neighborhood Satanists on Halloween.

Joe stopped within a little gathering of pines on the side of Route 3. He stared at the road.

"What?" I said, wondering what we were looking at.

He extended his arm and pointed like a prophet locating God.

"See him?" he whispered.

"No," I said, "who?"

"*Him!*" Joe pointed with all his fingers and thumbs, and I saw. There on the side of the road lay a huge porcupine. Dead.

"I *need* him," said Joe. "Help me get him."

Once more, I didn't hesitate: "Sure!" But I wondered, *Why?* On second thought, I said it: "Why?"

Joe answered with a symbol and a sound. He made his hand into a fist then stuck up his thumb. A classic thumbs up. Before I had time to give him a thumbs up in return, he made this sound: "Tsssssssssss," a sound I recognized immediately.

It was the sound of a wick burning. The sound of a bomb, its performance begun. Which meant Joe's hand was not a thumbs up at all. It was a bomb, his fist the bomb's body, his thumb the wick. I was a wiz at symbology even then.

"A bomb?" I said.

"A bomb," he said.

"But what do we need the porcupine for?"

He looked at me with pity, but then I figured it out, and my entire face peeled open into a crazy smile. He smiled back, his mouth a mirror of my own, which let me see how insanely happy I looked, and I loved it.

We were on the same page, and on that page:

A bomb and a porcupine.

The two would become one flesh, and then...

*And then!*

## Nine

Joe found his way to bombmaking innocently.

He got there on the gateway drug of model rockets. These are very fun. You light them, stand back, then watch them blast off and fly hundreds of feet into the air.

- Sometimes the rocket has a built-in camera that takes pictures of all the shingle damage on top of your house.

- Sometimes the rocket expels tiny paratroopers, which float down like airborne diseases into the yards of neighbors you hate.
- Sometimes the rocket explodes and burns on the launchpad. As a reflex action, you shout, "Shit!" Then Mother, who you invited outside to watch the launch, reflexively punishes you even though you used the word at the appropriate time and volume.

It didn't take Joe long to do all of these things, to reach the end of everything rockets in his price range could do. So, he started removing the rocket engines, cutting them open and using their powder to make his very first bombs.

He filled tennis balls and soda cans with rocket powder, and though these loosely packed explosives flared more than they boomed, he was happy. So was I; something about bombs prompted Joe to defy elder brother codes of conduct and include me.

I was there for the tennis balls and soda cans, and I was there after them, keeping the secret.

All bombs were between us. No friends allowed.

Brothers only.

There was no other way to keep the work safe from the meddlesome syndicate of caring parents.

Fine by me: I had my big brother all to myself.

At Walmart, Joe and I used lawnmower money to buy many, many rocket engines. We bought them all. The cashier said, "You boys shootin' off rockets?"

In unison, we said, "Yes."

Yes, we were happy with our ball- and can-bombs, but like all happiness, it didn't last.

We watched the little booms and flares with sighs and wandering minds, dreaming, hoping for a new pathway, one that would allow for the width and weight of greater destruction.

Then it happened.

The evolution of Joe's bombs experienced a leap, a beneficial mutation. He discovered a new material begging to be used. It was all around us, hiding in plain sight…

## Eight

See, we were BB gun boys. To our credit, we never killed animals. And we never shot people, though we admired those who did, the legendary boys who'd fought in the great BB gun wars and famously had BBs lodged within themselves, BBs traveling slowly toward their heroic hearts. One day, they would die of their fame.

Is there a better death?

The answer's no in the sense of never.

Joe and I restricted ourselves to shooting inanimate objects like road signs and glass bottles. We also shot slightly more animate objects, such as cars and trucks on Route 3.

We hid in the woods beside the big road like assassins, and to our credit, we only shot the ones that were, or looked like, the cars and trucks of people we hated.

All that shooting left behind heaps of empty $CO_2$ cartridges, the little steel containers made for holding compressed gas. BB propellent. What to do with such a bounty of scrap-metal waste?

This was the 90s, a time when the busybodies of the city were trying to save the planet. Their bullying finally reached the backcountry, and against our wills, we learned the word "recycling."

To spite the city, we took our stockpile of spent CO2 cartridges, and with a hacksaw, we turned them into a stockpile of homemade grenades.

"Recycle *this!*"

No more rocket powder, by the way, for it was weak. To explode metal, we needed the real thing: *gunpowder*. Where did we get it? Correct, the great provider. At Walmart, we bought kegs of Pyrodex gunpowder, the kind meant for black powder rifles.

The cashier said, "You boys goin' huntin'?"

We said, "Yes."

### Seven

The first thing Joe and I blew up was a tree. We used Dad's drill to make a hole in an innocent birch, inserted the bomb, lit the thing, then ran.

The explosion cruelly shivered the tree, which sprinkled down leaves in a sad shower, and the explosion knocked us over with laughter, self-love, and a level of unity we'd never felt before:

*Thank you, God, for these thy bombs. There's just something about them, Lord. They seem to make me and Joe… friends? I believe that's the word. We might actually be friends.*

Down came the tree, its remaining leaves hissing with surprise and rage, then the tree struck the ground with a "thud!" we felt in our joy-grinding teeth.

We hushed and were humbled by our success. And we wanted more. Not more humility. More success. Very soon, we found more.

## Six

Our next success came in the form of a bowling ball.

It had been given to us by a deacon at our church, a man everyone called Bud. I could imitate him *very well*. Bud was one of my classics. He had a weird way of talking, the weird so thick it was hard not to laugh while he talked, but we weren't laughing when Bud located my brother and I after church one Sunday and said, "I got something I want you boys to destroy."

We glanced at each other. *Does Bud know about the bombs? Or is this just a coincidence in addition to a sign of God's favor?*

Bud went to his car and came back with an aqua-colored bowling ball and said, "Drop it on a rock or hit it with axes. I don't care how you do it, I just want to see what's inside. Do we have a deal?"

It was clear: Bud had no idea about the bombs. It was magic and coincidence. In other words, God was with us.

"Deal," we said.

We set Bud's ball in the woods then locked ourselves in Joe's room and made a bomb. Yes, giggling all the time.

It's amazing how much giggling is involved in adventure work.

Mom knocked on the door and said, "Ready for lunch?"

We shouted, "Nothing!"

"What?"

"Oh," we said. "Yes."

After a lunch so healthy it was tasteless, we finished the bomb. Then into the woods we went. The bowling ball watched our approach while wearing an expression of wide-open dread.

Its instincts were correct: We weren't in the woods to bowl.

Joe slipped the bomb into the middle finger hole, and we immediately realized to our delight that we'd created a perfect replica of a *Looney Tunes* bomb. That cute, iconic sphere of death. Beautiful. We felt God's favor yet again.

Joe lit the wick, which looked like the bowling ball's middle finger aimed our way, then we ran for cover.

"Tsssssssssssssssssssssssssssssssss—"

"BOOM!"

We cried out our joy and sang, but then humility hushed us again: A humbling downpour of bowling ball bits and chunks struck the forest floor. We covered our heads, shut our eyes tight, and waited for pain, but not even a single nugget of shrapnel killed us.

Our faith increased: "For he shall give his angels charge over thee, to keep thee in all thy ways. They shall bear thee up in their hands, lest thou dash thy foot against a stone."

We stared at each other with faith so gigantic there wasn't room for much more God in us.

Meaning he needed me and Joe to make more room, to level up, to demo the dead ends of the chambers holding our faith.

God said, "Do all that is in thine heart."

Joe and I said, "Bombs is all that is in our hearts."

God nodded. "Do it."

Next Sunday, we delivered the bowling ball remains to Bud. He cradled a jagged hunk of aqua in his hands. What was inside his bowling ball? Nothing unusual. Turns out bowling balls are bowling balls all the way down.

But now he knew it, and he was moved to whispering: "Thank you, boys." Then he said something our Grampa often said: "You got three kinds of people." It was like Grampa talking through him. "You got people who make things happen, people who watch 'em happen, and people who wonder, 'What happened?'"

Bud held out the shrapnel. "You, boys... you *make* things happen!"

## Five

After this incredible triumph, Joe and I immediately made two other things happen:

> **ONE**: I delivered the "make things happen" speech daily, but in Bud's voice, getting closer and closer to perfection.
>
> **TWO**: Joe and I, destruction drunk, expanded our faith.

We started duct taping the $CO_2$-cartridge grenades to spray cans of WD-40.

At first, we tried a single can.

"BOOM!"

Not enough. Two cans.

"BA-BOOM!!"

More, damn it!

The Walmart cashier said, "That sure is a lot of WD-40. You boys lubricating lots of stuff?"

Again, we answered as one: "Yes."

Finally, we did the maximum, duct taping three WD-40 cans in a loving embrace around our grenade.

"*BA-BA-BA-BOOM!!!*"

It produced a fireball the size of a trailer truck.

After this masterpiece, we experienced a common setback: Bomber's block.

We were plumb out of ideas, and though no one knows what "plumb" means, it was true: We had nothing.

## Four

Joe and I became sullen and moody. We were boys with bombs but nothing to blow up. We languished. We shot signs and cars with our BB guns, but the thrill was gone. For a couple days we tried waiting for winter. In winter, we hoped to cut holes in the ice over Branch Pond and detonate bombs that would chase us with tsunamis of ice and poisonously cold water.

But that was winter. Years away.

And we couldn't wait.

We had tasted fire and power at levels far beyond the reach of mortal boys. We needed more. *Fast*. It had to be something new, unique, but also free, for we had spent all our cash on cans of lube.

So, Joe went out walking alone. He went to think, to dream. He walked the woods.

He walked the meadows and fields and the old woods roads.

He walked for so long, so many days and nights, he forgot about our nearness to friendship. Again, we were nothing but brothers. Again, I was younger and stupid.

Invisible.

Joe walked until he stumbled into a small assembly of pines on the edge of Route 3.

As cars and trucks and trailer trucks came and went, his eyes blurred and he saw an empty future, a future of zero adventure, for all adventurous things had been tried and were over. They were dust and ash.

Vanity of vanities.

But then an image cut through the blurry gloom. An image that would become the symbol of our childhood pride forever more.

It was a round object on the side of the road and as big as a basketball. Bigger. Big as the corpse of a basketball swollen in a river. Not only a round object, but a former creature. Reduced by death to a purposeless vessel...

*But it could have purpose again.*

It could carry something like life again. Would it mind? Would it mind donating its body to a certain kind of science? If it meant doing something like living one last time, or at least giving life to others, of course it wouldn't mind!

The great giggle began, and Joe ran for home. For help.

He ran for me.

## Three

The porcupine was very dead.

It had been struck by a thundering road warrior and left for very dead on the edge of Route 3.

It must have just happened, sometime in the night or early morning, because the porcupine was untouched by scavenging critters. Even the flies, those great gossips of carnage, didn't know. And whatever hit the porcupine, it had to have been a surgical strike, because apart from the swelling, he looked brand new.

"I *need* him," Joe said. "Help me get him." Then he explained: "Tsssssssssssssssssssss..."

*Now* I knew why he needed me. Not because of my speed or my asymmetrically developed rock-skipping arm. Not because of my knives either. Generally, Joe needed me because he had a new bomb in mind, praise God. Specifically, he needed me because of another skill I possessed:

I was always willing and able to do disgusting things.

- I dissected worms with my teeth.
- Hurled myself into the murkiest swamps, vanishing beneath the quilt of scum and duck itch.
- I used nosebleeds to plaster my torso in blood and look like a murdered boy.
- I did whatever got a laugh or was considered impressive or extreme, you name it.

Therefore, Joe assumed I'd have no trouble collecting a dead animal from the side of the

road. He was right, and I was honored.

That day, a few motorists of Route 3 witnessed something interesting. Take a look:

Two boys stand on the side of the dangerous road. One boy is doing nothing but laughing. The other, the small one, who is also laughing, carefully rolls a large porcupine corpse onto an orange plastic sled. Then he drags the sled off into the trees. The tall boy follows. He is laughing still and clapping and dancing.

I would give *anything* to see that moment in the hands of Norman Rockwell. Oh, Norman, paint me *my* America.

Once the porcupine was resting comfortably in our woods, it was time to build a bomb.

We ran to Joe's room and locked the door. He finessed the gunpowder into the cartridge while I watched. Seriousness descended as we focused on the deadly work. But our focus broke again and again when hilarity charged in, driven by a single image Joe and I shared:

A swollen porcupine with a wick sticking out of his belly.

The giggling was out of control.

A knock on the door.

*Mom.*

"Nothing!" we shouted.

"What?" she said. "I made popcorn."

"Oh!"

We waited for her to go back downstairs. We followed, decimated the low-sodium, no-butter, no-nonsense popcorn without speaking, then hurried back to Joe's room.

When the bomb was done at last, Joe said, "Dan."

"What?"

"Get a knife."

A tear came out of my eye. It's greatly satisfying for knife lovers to hear "get a knife," because then we get to say, "Which one?"

Joe said, "Pick one you don't like very much."

I dug to the bottom of my one-ton military knife-box and retrieved a horn-handled, rusty piece of trash. I didn't like it very much, but that day, for a glorious moment or two, I loved it. It came through beautifully, getting its hands dirty in ways my other, finer knives would never dream of.

Joe put the bomb in a backpack, I did the same with my knife, then we ran: down the hall, down the stairs, out the front door, around the corner of the house, but there, we were stopped.

Not by Mom.

Not by the law.

We were stopped by the sudden appearance of a friend, Joe's friend Paul Adams. He was standing in our driveway.

*On a bomb day.*

## Two

It didn't make any sense. Joe and I had told *no one*.
And yet, there was Paul.
The wild one.
He was an impulsive boy:

- Out of nowhere, he would scream like a dying rabbit, scaring everyone.
- He loved seizing people in bear hugs at random and swinging them around.
- He also went through seasons of unpredictable headbutting. Paul was my first concussion.
- Also, sometimes, he just appeared in driveways like mean magic.

I looked at Joe with accusatorial eyes, which shouted, *You TOLD him?!*

His eyes looked the same way, but he wasn't accusing me—he couldn't. Paul wasn't *my* friend—but Joe was accusing someone, something, maybe the Universe. Bottom line,

if *we* hadn't invited Paul, and we *had not*, how had he known to materialize in our driveway?

My only guess is this:

Paul had experienced a feeling. While biking in the neighborhood, he'd felt Joe's bomb excitement, a feeling that said, "*Paul.*"

"Here I am," Paul said.

"Go to Joe's. *Now.*"

You hear about this when it comes to tragedy. A mother wakes in the middle of the night knowing one of her children has been in a car accident. A son suddenly goes weak in the knees. His father, half the world away, is gone.

He *felt* it.

If this can happen because of horrible things, it can happen because of good things too. For example, Paul standing in our driveway uninvited on the day of the porcupine bomb.

Why hadn't our earlier bombs drawn friends?

It's simple:

Those bombs had been great, but none of them had produced near-deadly levels of joy in Joe, the only kind of joy loud enough to summon passing friends so they could stand in our driveway, block us, and ask, "What are you guys doing?"

Joe answered, and because he couldn't wait another second, he decided not to lie: "Paul," he said, "what you're about to see… you can never tell anyone."

I sighed bitterly, internally. *So, Paul will be joining us.*

I didn't mind Paul, but he would change everything. The Joe who was kind when it was just us and bombs would be gone. The Joe who was especially cruel when accompanied by friends would replace my Joe, and I'd go back to being infinitely young and dumb. No longer would I be half-owner of the bomb. It didn't matter that I'd been there for all the others, for the building of this one, or that my knife was needed, or that I'd collected the porcupine and dragged him into the woods.

All irrelevant.

The bomb belonged to Joe and Paul now, and I was just lucky to be along for the ride.

Paul promised he wouldn't tell a soul, and Joe said, "Correct. Because if you ever do, you're a liar, and you'll burn in hell."

"Of course," said Paul, smiling. He lived and loved a high-stakes life.

Promises and threats made, we ran for the family woods, and as we ran, Joe looked over at me and grinned, something he'd never done in the presence of a visiting friend before. Suddenly, I had a feeling that maybe I'd been wrong.

Maybe Joe was still my Joe somehow, even with a friend nearby.

We led Paul into the dark woods. Then Joe and I stopped, and with the gravity of men of God, we pointed.

"What?" said Paul. Then he *saw*.

The porcupine made him start jumping up and down, then, for some reason, he screamed, "The harvest!" Next, he screamed, "Where'd you get it?!"

"Route 3." Joe glanced at me. "Dan got it."

To be publicly acknowledged by Joe made me wild like Paul. I took out and flourished my rusty knife, gleefully stabbing invisible enemies while Joe explained why we had the porcupine.

The explanation was simple:

Recycling.

Joe held the bomb lovingly in his hand and we stood in a ring around it. As we looked back and forth between the bomb and the porcupine, something wonderful happened: We became extremely forgetful. We forgot we were boys with pasts and possible futures. Memory, regret, and dread of the unknown all went away, leaving us simply children through and through, beings who in that moment were forever beyond the reach of time.

Maybe.

But I can say for sure there was nowhere else we wanted to be, which is another way of saying nowhere else existed.

We were the only boys on Earth, standing on the only place on Earth.

And I was welcome there, because in that place and at that time, Joe was more than my brother.

He was my friend.

At the end of this little séance of ours, I bragged that I would be the one performing the bomb-injection surgery.

Paul alone was jealous. He looked at Joe. "*I* can do it."

"Dan's doing it," Joe said, and then to me, "It's *time*."

I, Knife Boy, proud as the Devil, walked my blade to the porcupine.

I can still see him lying in a sunbeam, though there was none, not in those dark woods. But still, the shine was there, the glow of God's support, which had led us to model rockets and $CO_2$ cartridges and bowling balls and WD-40 and not dying and finally to the porcupine, and all without Mom and Dad knowing.

Praise God, from whom all blessings flow.

My plan was to drive the knife's point into the porcupine's exposed belly until the blade broke through, making a doorway for the bomb.

Which means you're asking, "Why didn't you guys just use the mouth or anus?"

Good question. Both were available. Either would have sufficed.

We snubbed the mouth and anus because we wanted that classic bomb look, the one we'd achieved with Bud's bowling ball: a wick sticking from the top of a globular form, not lamely sprouting from lips or anus, no matter how convenient and more respectful that would have been.

I touched the knife's point to the skin and pushed down. It went down and down, deeper and deeper, but the skin refused to split open.

I pushed until it made me sick. I gagged and wobbled off. Though I was the king of disgusting things, I apparently had a weak stomach when it came to porcupine postmortems. This weakness activated Paul.

He'd been watching the operation closely. The moment I stepped away, he said, "Nope!" then he guided me forcefully back to my work. He patted me on the back hard enough to put lights in my eyes, and I rallied. Not only because of Paul's encouragement, but because of *why* he'd encouraged me instead of taking the knife out of my hand...

He was following Joe's orders: *Dan's doing it.* Another way of saying, *Dan can do it, Dan can do anything he puts his mind to, because he can, and because I, his big brother and friend, said so.*

*That's why.*

Kneeling at the porcupine's side, I touched blade to belly again. But this time, instead of trying to stab, I sawed the blade back and forth.

It worked.

The skin gave way. It opened.

While I sawed on, Paul guarded my morale with words sacred to him. He quoted the Chef Boyardee beef ravioli commercial that was famous that year. It depicted a filthy boy in a jungle setting attacking marines one by one and stealing cans of ravioli from their backpacks. At the end, the boy, his mouth wreathed in ravioli gore, looks at the camera and says, "Mmm, *beefy.*"

Paul bellowed this special blessing over me as I worked: "Mmm! BEEFY!"

My blade opened the belly wide, and we saw the marvelous mystery of guts. Immediately after that, we had to slap our hands over our mouths and noses. The stench was incredible. Think of the worst smell you've ever smelled, now put it inside a porcupine overnight then bake him in summer for half the morning. We giggled, gagged, and stumbled around like blissfully gassed men.

When we recovered, Joe approached the porcupine. He held the bomb by the wick with his index finger and thumb then lowered it down and down until the bright metal of the cartridge met the open mouth of the wound.

In it went, sinking with surprising ease and silence, until there was no bomb left to see, only a stiff gray wick sticking out of the belly.

Right away, we saw what we had done. We'd transformed a porcupine into an honest-to-goodness bomb and much more: the grandest *Looney Tunes* bomb ever crafted. We laughed, we shouted in each other's faces. We wept and praised the Lord for his support, for the blind eye he'd turned our way so lovingly, letting us live like he wanted us to: with all our heart, soul, mind, and strength, amen.

## One

Finally, it was time to light the bomb. This privilege, of course, belonged to Joe. He was our leader, and no one questioned his right.

We moved with him in a giggling cluster and crouched with him at the porcupine's side. His arm went out, lighter in hand, and the sound of the lighter was this: "Scritch! Scritch!"

Like I said before, the excitement of lighting a bomb is the excitement of making wishes come true. Oh, how it electrifies the senses.

"Scritch!" said the lighter again.

Your heightened senses think a pin-drop is a gunshot, and your heart becomes a gorilla with a kettledrum.

"Scritch!"

Your eyes widen. You must see everything or die, and you do.

"Scritch!"

You wish for more eyes, all over your body like those monsters in the Bible who day and night stare at heaven's lethal dynamo: God Himself.

"Scritch! Scritch!" and suddenly, the wick caught fire:

"Tsssssssssssssss!"

And we, the boys who had been all eyes, ears, noses, giggles, and chattering teeth became running boys. For our lives. Running for trees, rocks, and rivers—"Mountains, fall on us!"—whatever would hide us from the blast.

We hid.
We waited our seven to ten seconds…
And then,
*and then…*

### *BOOM!!!!*

We screamed in tune with the sound, then up we jumped, tripping over our adrenaline-trembling feet, racing for ground zero —

Too soon!

We found ourselves caught in a lunatic rain of quills and old blood.

We became bloody, quill-adorned apocalypse boys.

We rejoiced.

And then, we found our porcupine.

He was spread out in all directions. Arms here. Legs there. Head, nowhere. Guts?

*Gone!*

The bomb had done its work well, and we danced. Yet we were wrong. Not in our dancing but in our guess. The guts weren't gone. Not quite.

Above the blast, hanging from a branch like a stork's sack of life, there was a green pouch packed with intestines. It swung not in the breeze, for there was no breeze in the suddenly warm woods. It wagged back and forth from the momentum of its sky journey. Either that or it wagged with the rocking of our queasy brains.

I watched the guts swing.

So did Joe.

Paul too.

And just as we opened our mouths to laugh so we wouldn't puke, we were struck by a misty blast wave of stink so thick it filled our mouths with porcupine gravy, and up and down the line of us, we gagged and spit and gulped our vomit down, and we laughed, died laughing until we were lying on the floor of the woods, anointed with blood, slayed by joy.

And then I offered my brother the sacred words:

"You got three kinds of people: You got people who make things happen, people who watch 'em happen, and people who wonder, 'What happened?'"

We shrieked and cheered because of how good my Bud voice had become.

Then Joe turned to me and said, "What about us? Which are we?"

He was asking.

He meant it.

I cried out, "We *make* things happen!" then I reached my bloody hands for the sky and shouted, "For we are *BEEFY!*"

And we all died again.

The End

your doodles, memories, illustrations, story ideas...

# Afterword

Thank you for reading this, a whole book of it. There are other things you could have been doing:
- thanking your parents and grandparents for their love and sacrifices, and saying "I love you" one last time
- spending minutes and hours with your spouse
- minutes and hours with your children so they grow up knowing deep in their hearts that they are loved
- donating blood
- rescuing animals
- going to therapy
- giving to charity

Thank you for reading my book instead of doing these things. It means a lot to me. It also means a lot to your family and to the people in need, not in a good way, but meaning is meaning.

And since you spent the time here that you didn't spend there, that makes us friends. Buddies.

And what do buddies do?

They share stories.

I hope the freakeries of my childhood call out to the freakeries of yours. One wolf gets another wolf howling, then they all howl.

That's what I'm talking about.

Guys, I love stories more than anything else. Stories are why I don't pray for world peace. Stories are world peace. What do I mean? I mean you and me, all of us, sitting together, getting the stories going and keeping them going, round and round the gigantic worldwide circle of us.

Here's a picture of this in action:

When I'm back home in Maine, when Mom and Dad and Grammy and Grampa are tempted to talk politics, babies, money, home and auto maintenance, and illness, I do my best to steer these old story vaults in the right direction:

- "Dad, tell about the time you accidentally trespassed in the cabin of a murderer…"
- "Grammy, tell about the time you beat up a rampaging pig with nothing but a two-by-four…"
- "Mom, tell about the time you patrolled the family's blueberry fields armed with a gun and a cat…"
- "Grampa, tell about the time you froze the lining of your stomach in an ice cream eating contest and won and almost died… about the time you caught a dog in midair, a dog flying toward dad's throat to kill him… about the time you pruned the old elm tree with a shotgun… the time you and a pack of friends rolled a model-T Ford down a hill, destroying it… about the time you performed the Heimlich on a sheep, firing the obstruction, an apple, out of the sheep like the bullet from a hilarious gun, but also killing the sheep… tell me about everything…"

Now it's your turn, friends and neighbors:
- Tell about the time you saw a ghost…
- Tell about the strangest thing you ever saw an animal do…
- Tell about a person you met who scared the crap out of you…
- about the most dramatic vomit session of your life…
- about the weirdest thing anyone ever said to you…
- about the time you almost died…
- or did die, then came back…
- about the dumbest thing you ever said
- ever did…

Tell me about everything, and send it all here:
daniel.williams737@gmail.com

Now, get back to that neglected family of yours so you can give them this book. May they abandon you as you abandoned them, then you can all come back together again and be friends, family. In other words, you can tell stories.

Love, your friend,

Dan

your doodles, memories, illustrations, story ideas...

# Acknowledgments

Mom and Dad, thank you for your love, encouragement, and faith. Thank you for freedom from the beginning. Thank you, Joe, my big brother and the villain of this book; thank you for being a good sport about me publishing this without your permission. Meg, my little sister, thank you for wanting to be my friend so badly that you've put up with being my friend all these years.

Thank you to my grandparents, Grammy Nancy and Grampa Fred. You fill my life with love, laughter, magic, and stories. You're the moon to me, the woods, and the ocean.

Thank you, Andrew Calvetti, for all the walkabouts and dream talks, for reading this book when it was still forming, and for saying this about your nightly readings: "It's a wonderful feeling knowing the book's waiting for me, and it's going to be a good time."

Thank you, Josiah Everett, for reading the book and offering encouragement. Thank you for all the story talks, wisdom, and laughter.

Thank you, band of brothers: Matt Kickasola, Rut Etheridge, Joel Ward, and Dan Cross—in some other dimension, we're all kicking around in the same womb. I love you guys.

Thank you, Lynda Szabo, Shirley Kilpatrick, and Frederic S. Durbin for being wind to the sails, sending the book where it needed to go.

Thank you, my Medium friends, who have been saying, "Where's the book?" for a long time. Friends, here it is. I hope you dig it.

Thank you Manette Ansay and Rikki Ducornet, story shepherds.

Thank you, Dayana Stetco, my teacher, friend, and *il miglior fabbro*.

Thank you, Keith Martel, for your Falls City Press, for saying yes to this book, and for being a mighty force and fortress of "yes," guidance, and patience.

Thank you to my students who heard so many of these stories when I should have been teaching. You fine folks gave me the impression that the stories were worth writing down. Thank you.

Sawyer, my son, my boy, fantastic spirit creature of my heart, thank you for loving my stories. Your laughter has said to me so many times, "Tell it again."

And Mindy, my wife and blood brother, my Tabitha King, thank you for loving and liking me and for reading everything I ever put before your eyes. Thank you for your brilliant suggestions, questions, and critiques. Thank you for your hope. You're my firefly, my will-o-the-wisp, my space family, and good witch of the planet tree.

*Imzadi.*

# About the Author

Dan Williams is a child rotting in time's river, a kid-thing bloated to adult-sized features, and he has no prospects. So, he teaches, writes stories, and draws people without their permission. His teachers called him unteachable; his preachers called him irredeemable; and his parents said, "Not everyone's going to be good at life."

**Find, Follow, and Friend Dan:**

| | |
|---|---|
| Substack: | danielwilliams964078 |
| Instagram: | danielwilliams6098 |
| TikTok | daniel.williams37 |
| Medium: | danielwilliams737 |
| Spotify Podcast: | Misbehaving In Maine |
| YouTube: | danielwilliams5251 |
| Mastodon: | danielwilliams737 |
| X: | dpwillia2 |
| Facebook: | Daniel Williams |

www.ingramcontent.com/pod-product-compliance
Lightning Source LLC
Chambersburg PA
CBHW030229100526
44583CB00013BA/619